Yorkshire Family Histories and Pedigrees

Stuart A. Raymond

Yorkshire: The Genealogists Library Guide 6

Published by the
Federation of Family History Societies (Publications) Ltd.,
2-4 Killer Street, Ramsbottom, Bury,
Lancashire, BL0 9BZ, U.K.

Copies also obtainable from:
S.A. & M.J. Raymond, P.O.Box 35, Exeter, EX1 3YZ, U.K.

First published 2000

ISBN: 1 86006 112 5

ISSN: 1033-2065

Printed and bound by The Alden Group, London and Northamton.

Contents

Front cover: Leeds Town Hall

Introduction

This bibliography is intended primarily for genealogists. It is, however, hoped that it will also prove useful to historians, librarians, archivists, research students, and anyone else interested in the history of Yorkshire. It is intended to be used in conjunction with my *English genealogy: a bibliography,* with the other volumes of *Yorkshire: the genealogists library guide,* and with the companion volumes in the *British genealogical library guides* series. A full list of these volumes currently in print appears on the back cover.

Published sources of information on Yorkshire genealogy are listed in volumes 1-5 of *Yorkshire: the genealogists library guide;* this volume lists works devoted to the history of specific families, together with collections of pedigrees, biographical dictionaries, diaries & letters, and Yorkshire heraldry. It includes published books and journal articles, but excludes the innumerable notes and queries to be found in the many family history society journals, except where their content is of importance. Where I have included such notes, replies to them are cited in the form 'see also', with no reference to the names of respondents. I have also excluded extracts from newspapers, and works which have not been published. Where possible, citations are accompanied by notes indicating the period covered, the locality/ies in which the families concerned dwelt, and other pertinent information. I have physically examined almost every item listed here; those which have not been seen are annotated 'not seen', as I have not been able to check the correct title or the contents. Pedigrees and family histories contained in works on other genealogical topics, and listed in other volumes of this library guide, are excluded here, since all six volumes are intended to be used together.

Be warned: just because information has been published, it does not necessarily follow that it is accurate. I have not made any judgement on the accuracy of most works listed: that is up to you.

Anyone who tries to compile a totally comprehensive bibliography of Yorkshire is likely to fall short of his aim. The task is almost impossible, especially if the endeavour is made by one person. That does not, however, mean that the attempt should not be made. This book is as comprehensive as I have been able to make it. However, usefulness, rather than compre-hensiveness, has been my prime aim — and this book would not be useful to anyone if its publication were to be prevented by a vain attempt to ensure total comprehensiveness. I am well aware that there are likely to be omissions, especially in view of the fact that, given constraints of time and money, it has not been possible for me to visit all of the large number of libraries with substantial collections on Yorkshire's history. Each of them may well possess works not held anywhere else. The identification of such works is not, however, a major aim of this bibliography. Rather, my purpose has been to enable you to identify works which are mostly readily available.

Some titles you may be able to purchase; all can be found in libraries throughout the English-speaking world. You can check the holdings of many libraries via their catalogues on the internet; alternatively, if your local library does not hold a particular book, the librarian should be able to tell you where to find it – and, as a last resort, may be able to borrow it for you via the inter-library loan network, irrespective of whether you live in London or San Francisco. The libraries of family history societies are also worth checking – even if they are far distant from Yorkshire: for example, the Genealogical Society of Victoria, in Melbourne, has a good collection of books on English genealogy. Some family history societies offer a postal borrowing service; others may be willing to check a particular book for you. It is also worth joining one of the genealogical newsgroups or mailing lists on the internet; other members may hold the books you need, and be willing to check them for you.

If you are an assiduous researcher, you may well come across items I have missed. If you do, please let me know, so that they can be included in the next edition.

The work of compiling this bibliography has depended heavily on the resources of the libraries I have used. These included the local studies collections in the public libraries of Bradford, Doncaster, Hull, Leeds, Sheffield, and York, the Brotherton Library at the University of Leeds, the British Library, the Society of Genealogists, Guildhall Library, the University and the Central Library in Bristol, the University of Exeter library and the Exeter Public Library in Exeter. I have also used the resources of a number of family history societies, and am particularly grateful to the societies for Devon, Cornwall, Somerset & Dorset, Sheffield and Ripon/Harrogate. All these institutions deserve my thanks, as does John Perkins, who read and commented on an early draft of the book. Paul Raymond and Mark Gant typed the manuscript, and Bob Boyd saw the book through the press. I am grateful too to the officers of the Federation of Family History Societies, whose support is vital for the continuation of this series. I am also grateful to the Yorkshire Archaeological Society, who employed me as their librarian between 1975 and 1979, and thus launched my interest in Yorkshire genealogy and bibliography. My thanks also to my wife Marjorie.

Stuart A. Raymond

Abbreviations

B.A.	*Bradford antiquary*
B.S.H.S.	*Bulletin of the Saddleworth Historical Society*
B.T.	*Banyan tree: journal of the East Yorkshire Family History Society*
C.R.S.	*Catholic Record Society*
C.T.L.H.S.B.	*Cleveland and Teeside Local History Society*
C.Y.D.F.H.S.J.	*City of York & District Family History Society journal*
C.Y.D.F.H.S.N.	*City of York & District Family History Society newsletter*
Cameo	*Cameo: Morley & District Family History Group newsletter*
Don. Anc.	*Doncaster ancestor*
E.Y.L.H.S.	East Yorkshire Local History Society series
F.H.S.	Family History Society
F.S.	*Flowing stream: journal of Sheffield & District Family History Society*
H.& D.F.H.S.J.	*Huddersfield & District Family History Society journal*
J.Cl.F.H.S.	*Journal of the Cleveland Family History Society*
K.D.F.H.S.J.	*Keighley & District Family History Society journal*
M.G.H.	*Miscellanea genealogica et heraldica*
N. & Q.	*Notes and queries: a quarterly magazine ... South Yorkshire ...*
N.H.	*Northern History*
N.Y.C.R.O.P.	North Yorkshire County Record Office publications
O.W.R.	*Old West Riding*
P.R.H.A.S.	*Papers, reports, etc., read before the Halifax Antiquarian Society*
R. & D.F.H.S.N.	*Rotherham and District Family History Society newsletter*
R.H.	*Ripon Historian*
T.E.R.A.S.	*Transactions of the East Riding Archaeological Society*
T.Hal.A.S.	*Transactions of the Halifax Archaeological Society*

T. Hunter A.S.	*Transactions of the Hunter Archaeological Society*
T.R.S.	*Teesdale Record Society [proceedings]*
T.S.	Thoresby Society
Wh.N.	*Wharfedale newsletter: the journal of the Wharfedale Family History Group*
Y.A.J.	*Yorkshire archaeological journal*
Y.A.S., F.H.P.S.S.	Yorkshire Archaeological Society. Family History and Population Studies Section
Y.A.S., F.H.P.S.S.N.	*Yorkshire Archaeological Society. Family History and Population Studies Section newsletter*
Y.A.S., R.S.	Yorkshire Archaeological Society. Record Series
Y.C.M.	*Yorkshire county magazine*
Y.F.H.	*Yorkshire family historian*
Y.F.H.S.N.	*York Family History Society newsletter*
Y.G.	*Yorkshire genealogist*
Y.N.Q. I.	*Yorkshire notes & queries* [1888-90]
Y.N.Q. II.	*Yorkshire notes & queries* [1905-9]

Bibliographic Presentation

Authors' names are in SMALL CAPITALS. Book and journal titles are in *italics.* Articles appearing in journals, and essays, *etc.,* forming only parts of books, are in inverted commas. Volume numbers are shown in **bold,** and the individual numbers of journals may be shown in parentheses. In the case of articles, further figures indicate page numbers. Book titles are normally followed by the place of publication (except where this is London, which is omitted), the name of the publisher, and the date of publication.

1. PEDIGREE COLLECTIONS

A. *Heraldic Visitations*

The heraldic visitations of the 16th and 17th centuries, during which members of the gentry were required to produce proof of their right to heraldic arms, resulted in the production of numerous collections of pedigrees, many of which have been published. The Surtees Society has brought together a number of these collections relating to the North of England as a whole, in:

DENDY, FREDERICK WALTER, ed. *Visitations of the North, or, some early heraldic visitations of, and collections of pedigrees relating to, the North of England.* Surtees Society **122**. 1912. 'Part I'. Contents: 'Heraldic visitation of the northern counties made in 1552 by William Harvey, Norroy King of Arms'; 'The only extant portion of an heraldic visitation of the northern counties made in 1558 by Laurence Dalton, Norroy King of Arms.' 'Heraldic pedigrees of the Northern counties collected in 1560 and 1561, probably by Lawrence Dalton, Norroy King of Arms, or his deputy.'

DENDY, FREDERICK WALTER, ed. *Visitations of the North, or, some early heraldic visitations of, and collections of pedigrees relating to, the North of England.* Surtees Society **133**. 1920. 'Part II'. Contents: 'Heraldic visitation of Yorkshire made in 1563 and 1564 by William Flower, Norroy King of Arms'. 'Heraldic pedigrees of Yorkshire and adjacent counties collected 1567 by William Flower, Norroy King of Arms'.

BLAIR, C.H. HUNTER, ed. *Visitations of the North, part III: a visitation of the North of England circa 1480-1500.* Surtees Society **144**. 1930.

[BLAIR, C.H. HUNTER], ed. *Visitations of the North, part IV: visitations of Yorkshire and Northumberland in A.D. 1575, and a book of arms from Ashmole ms. No 834.* Surtees Society **146**. 1932.

A number of other visitation returns have been seperately printed – some in more than one edition. These include:

1530

LONGSTAFFE, W.HYLTON DYER, ed. *Heraldic visitation of the northern counties in 1530 by Thomas Tonge, Norroy King of Arms, with an appendix of other heraldic documents relating to the north of England.* Surtees Society **41**. 1863.

1563-4

NORCLIFFE, CHARLES BEST, ed. *The visitation of Yorkshire in the years 1563 and 1564, made by William Flower, esquire, Norroy King of Arms.* Publications of the Harleian Society **16**. 1881.

1584-5

FOSTER, JOSEPH, ed. *The visitation of Yorkshire made in the years 1584/5, by Robert Glover, Somerset Herald, to which is added the subsequent visitation made in 1612 by Richard St. George, Norroy King of Arms, with several additional pedigrees, including 'the arms taken out of churches and houses at Yorkshire visitation, 1584/5', 'Sir William Fayrfax' booke of arms', and other heraldic lists, with copious indices.* Joseph Foster, 1875.

1665-6

DAVIES, ROBERT, ed. *The visitation of the county of York, begin in A°Dni. MDCLXV, and finished A°Dni. MDCLXVI, by William Dugdale, esqr; Norroy king of Arms.* Surtees Society **36**. 1859. Indexed in:

ARMYTAGE, GEO. J. *Index to the visitation of the county of York begun A.D. MDCLXVI, and finished A.D. MDCLXVI, by William Dugdale, esqr., Norroy King of Arms.* James Bain, 1872.

CLAY, J.W., ed. *Dugdale's visitation of Yorkshire, with additions.* 3 vols. Exeter: W. Pollard & Co., 1899-1917. Partly reprinted from: CLAY, J.W. 'Dugdale's visitation of Yorkshire, with additions', *Genealogist* N.S., **9-33**, 1893-1917, *passim*

PEACOCK, EDWARD 'An index to the Lincolnshire names found in the visitation of Yorkshire, 1665', *Lincolnshire notes and queries* **3**, 1893, 86-9.

Other works on visitation pedigrees include: 'List of the pedigrees contained in Wm. Paver's consolidated visitations of Yorkshire, being those taken in 1584, 1612 and 1665', *New England historical and genealogical register* **11**, 1857, 259-71.
FLETCHER, JOHN. 'Heraldic visitations', *J.Cl.F.H.S.* **5**(8), 1993, 21-8. General discussion, with lists of pedigrees for Cleveland.

B. *Other Pedigree Collection*

Yorkshire is fortunate in that a large number of antiquaries have compiled and published collections of pedigrees — although of course they mainly relate to gentle families. Important collections include:
CLAY, CHARLES, SIR. *Early Yorkshire families.* Y.A.S., R.S. **135**. 1973. Descents of almost 100 early medieval families; includes folded pedigrees of Gospatrick, Vernoil and Vescy.
CLAY, JOHN WILLIAM. *The extinct and dormant peerages of the northern counties of England.* James Nisbet & Co., 1913. Covers Co. Durham, Northumberland Cumberland, Westmorland, Lancashire and Yorkshire.
FOSTER, JOSEPH. *Pedigrees of the county families of Yorkshire.* 3 vols. W.Wilfred Head, 1874-5. Extensive; thousands of pedigrees. Those from Cleveland are listed in: SAMPSON, ALEX. 'Book review: *Pedigrees of Yorkshire families volume 2: North and East Ridings,* compiled by Joseph Foster', *J.Cl.F.H.S.* **4**(1), 1989, 16-18.
HUNTER, JOSEPH. *Familiae minorum gentium,* ed. John W. Clay. 4 vols. Publications of the Harleian Society 37-40. 1894-6. Includes innumerable pedigrees of Yorkshire, Derbyshire, Cheshire and Lancashire families. Continued by:
WALKER, J.W., ed. *Hunter's pedigrees: a continuation of Familiae minorum gentium, diligentia Josephi Hunter.* Publications of the Harleian Society **88**. 1936.
TAYLOR, R.V. 'Index to Yorkshire pedigrees', *Y.G.* **1**, 1888, 60-64. To Ayscough only completed.

WALKER, J.W., ed. *Yorkshire pedigrees.* 3 vols. Publications of the Harleian Society 94-6. 1942-4. From various collections. Indexed in: 'Yorkshire pedigrees', *J.Cl.F.H.S.* **4**(12), 1991, 18-20. Index covers A-F only.
'Surnames from birth briefs' [continued as 'Extracts from ancestry record charts'], *J.Cl.F.H.S., passim.*

Doncaster

PALGRAVE, DEREK A. 'Prominent families in Doncaster Deanery', *Don. Anc.* **1**(3), 1981, 59-65. Lists numerous pedigrees in Hunter's *South Yorkshire.*

East Riding

HAWKESBURY, LORD. *Some East Riding families.* Hull: William Andrews & Co., 1899. Reprinted from *T.E.R.A.S.* **7**, 1899. Discussion of the history of families recorded in the heraldic visitations.

Eckington

GARRATT, H.J.H. 'Deduced genealogies from the Eckington court rolls now in Sheffield Archives', *F.S.* **13**(1), 1992, 16-17; **13**(2), 1992, 41-6.

Sheffield

HALL, T.WALTER. *Sheffield pedigrees.* Sheffield: J.W. Northend, 1915. 16 folded pedigrees.

York

PAVER, WILLIAM. *Pedigrees of families of the city of York.* York: R. Sunter, et al, 1842. Brief.
HAYWOOD, LINDA. 'Murray's York pedigrees', *C.Y.D.F.H.S.N.* **17**, 1988, 7-9. Discussion of a collection of manuscript pedigrees at York Reference Library, with list.

2. HERALDRY.

A. General

Heraldry can prove to be a useful supplement to genealogy. Much heraldic information is to be found on monumental inscriptions; these are dealt with in vol 2, section 2 of *Yorkshire: the genealogists library guide.*
The only general survey of Yorkshire coats of arms is:

TURNER, J.HORSFALL. *The coats of arms of the nobility & gentry of Yorkshire.* Idle: John Wade, 1911.
For a brief work on armorial seals, see:
CLAY, C.T. 'Some Yorkshire armorial seals', *Y.A.J.* **36**, 1944-7, 47-62.
Notes on 15 grants of arms are provided in: 'Grants of arms', *Y.A.J.* **18**, 1904-5, 342-52. 109-22, 232-40 & 342-52.
A handful of funeral certificates are printed in:
'Funeral certificates', *Y.A.J.* **12**, 1893, 402-4.
For Matthew Wentworth, 1637, William Ingleby, 1636, John Louell, 1637, Andrew Agar, 1637, Francis Stringer, 1637 and William Richards, 1637.
A number of works provide information on heraldry in particular localities:

Cleveland
BROWN, THOMAS H. *Coats of arms in Cleveland.* Middlesborough: Teeside Museums and Art Galleries service, 1973.

East Riding
COLLIER, CARUS VALE, & SCOTT-GATTY, A.S. 'The East Riding portion of an heraldic ms relating to Yorkshire,' *T.E.R.A.S.* **9**, 1902, 87-108. Arms of the gentry, *temp* Elizabeth .

Halifax
BRETTON, R. 'Local heraldry', *T.Hal.A.S.* 1929, 33-114; 1944, 49-62; 1958, 77-89. Notes on the coats of arms of Halifax families.

B. Family Heraldry

Agar
See Wentworth

Aldeburgh
DUCKETT, GEORGE, SIR. 'Arms of Aldeburgh (or Aldeburgh)', *Y.A.J.* **6**, 1881, 420-24.

Armytage
'Arms of Armytage and Wentworth', *M.G.H.* 4th series **5**, 1913, 16-18. Includes pedigrees, 12-18th c.

Aton
ELLIS, A.S. 'On the arms of de Aton', *Y.A.J.* **12**, 1893, 263-5. Medieval

Bainbridge
PETCHEY, W.J. 'A Ripon armorial, 10. Bainbridge. 11. Savage', *R.H.* **2**(6), 1994, 137-40.

Beckwith
PETCHEY, W.J. 'A Ripon armorial, 9. Beckwith of Clint, *R.H.* **2**(4), 1993, 84-8.

Blackett
PETCHEY, W.J. 'A Ripon armorial 13. Blackett of Newby Hall', *R.H.* **2**(10), 1995, 252-5.

Bullock
WILSON, R.E. 'The coat of arms of the Bullock family in Greenhill Hall, and the Bullock family', *T. Hunter A.S.* **9**(1), 1964, 1-7. See also **9**(2), 1966, 116. Includes pedigree, 15-17th C.

Clifford
BLUNDELL, JAMES. 'A mysterious Clifford quarter', *Coat of arms* **8**, 1966-7, 177-82. Medieval.

Conyers
See Norton

Cooke
COOKE, WILLIAM BRYAN *The sieze quartiers of the family of Bryan Cooke, esq., of Owston, Hafod-y-Wern and Gwysaney, and of Frances his wife, daughter and heir of Philip Puleston ...* Privately printed, 1857. Includes folded pedigree, 17-19th c.
'Grant of arms to John Cooke, 1653', *Fragmenta genealogica* **13**, 1909, 1. Of Giggleswick.

Crosland
PETCHEY, W.J. 'A Ripon armorial, 12.
Crosland of Newby', *R.H.* 2(8), 1994,
202-3.

Cullum
'Grant of arms to Dame Mary Cullum, only
daughter of Robert Hanson of Normanton,
Co. York, 1793', *M.G.H.* 2nd series 5, 1894,
66. Folded facsimile.

Ebblewhite
See Heblethwaite

Ellerker
'Grant of crest to Sir Ralph Ellerker,
Knight', *Genealogist* 1, 1877, 290-91. 1546.

Farrer
BRETTON, ROWLAND. 'A Farrer coat of
arms', *Coat of arms* 8, 1964-5, 73-4. Of
Halifax.

Fayrfax
'Sir William Fayrfax's book of arms of
Yorkshire', *Y.C.M.* 2, 1892, 210-20.

Green
BRETTON, ROWLAND. 'Arms of Green, or
Horton', *Coat of arms* 7, 1962-3, 342-4.
Includes confirmation of grant of arms to
Ann Horton of Barkisland, 1725.

Grene
'Grant of arms to William Grene, 17 July, 9
Henry VII', *M.G.H.* 2nd series 5,1894, 360.
Of Essex and Yorkshire.

Hanson
BRETTON, ROWLAND. 'A Commonwealth
grant of arms', *Coat of arms* 9, 1966-7,
261-3. Hanson family of Woodhouse.

Harrison
HENSLOWE, CAPTAIN. 'Armorial bookplate:
Thomas Harrison of Copgrove, Co. York,
esq., 1698', *M.G.H.* 2nd series 4, 1892, 168.
17-18th c.

Heber
FLETCHER, W.G.D. 'Grant of arms and crest to
Raynold Heber, of Marton in Craven,
1569', *Genealogist* N.S., 27, 1911, 222-3.

Heblethwaite
EBBELWHITE, ERNEST ARTHUR. 'Heblethwaite,
or Ebblethwaite', *M.G.H.* 3rd series 2,
1898, 17. Arms, 16-17th c.

Horton
See Green

Ingleby
See Wentworth

Jackson
'Grant of arms to Charles Jackson,
Doncaster', *M.G.H.* N.S., 4, 1884, 37. 1854.

Jessopp
'Grant of arms to Richard Jessopp of
Broomehall, Yorks, 1575', *M.G.H.* 5th
series 8, 1932-4, 172.

Lawevell
'Grant of crest to William Lawevell alias
Wombwell of Wombwell, 1565', *M.G.H.* 5th
series 7, 1929-31, 357.

Lawson
'Grant of crest to Ralph Lawson of Burgh,
Co. York 1592', *M.G.H.* N.S., 3, 1880, 29-30.

Lewis
'Grant of arms to John Lewis of Doncaster ',
M.G.H. 5th series 3, 1918-19, 193. 1586.

Louell
See Wentworth

Maltby
VERRILL, D.MALTBY. 'Maltby arms', *Notes
and queries* 155, 1928, 82-3. See also 121;
156, 1929, 462; 159, 1930, 195.

Manf(i)eld
'Diploma of the crest of Lancelot Manfeld,
1563', *New England historical &
genealogical register* 4, 1850, 141-2. Of
Skirpenbeck.
'Grant of a crest to Lancelot Manfield of
Skirpenbeck, Co. York', *M.G.H.* 5th series
3, 1918-19, 146. 1563; includes brief
pedigree.

Markenfield
PETCHEY, WILLIAM. 'A Ripon armorial, 1.
Markenfield: the origin of a coat of arms',
R.H. 1(1), 1988, 11-12.

Marmion
PETCHEY, WILLIAM. 'A Ripon armorial, II: Marmion. The nature of early armory', *R.H.* 1(2), 1988, 10-12.

Miniott
P[ETCHEY], W.J. 'A Ripon armorial III: Miniott', *R.H.* 1(3), 1990, 10-11.

Moustiers
PETCHEY, W.J. 'A Ripon armorial, 7. Moustiers or Musters; Wandesford', *R.H* 1(9), 1992, 13-15. 1(10), 1992, 10-14.

Norcliffe
'Grant of arms to Thomas Norcliffe', *Genealogist* 6, 1881, 35-6. 1612.

Norton
PETCHEY, W.J. 'A Ripon armorial, VI: the Norton Blackamoor', *R.H.* 1(7), 1992, 16-17.
PETCHEY, W.J. 'A Ripon armorial, V. Norton and Norton Conyers', *R.H.* 1(6), 1991, 13-14.

Pigott
'A Ripon armorial, IV. Pigott', *R.H.* 1(4), 1990, 13.

Richards
See Wentworth

Robotham
'Grant of arms and crest to Robert Robotham of Raskyll, Co. York, gent, 1560', *M.G.H.* 2nd series 1, 1886, 269-70.

Rodes
'Confirmation of arms by Robert Cooke, Clarenceux, to William Rodes of Skyrket, Co. York, 1585', *M.G.H.* 2nd series 3, 1890, 293.

Savage
See Bainbridge

Smithson
'Grant of arms to Sr. Hugh Smithson, kt., & Bart., 1663', *Genealogist* 1, 1877, 137.

Stringer
See Wentworth

Walker
'Grants and confirmations of arms and crest', *M.G.H.* 5th series 10, 1938, 101-3. Includes Walker of Yorkshire, 1562.

Wandesford
See Moustiers

Waterhouse
BRETTON, ROWLAND. 'Waterhouse coats of arms', *Coat of arms* 10, 1968-9, 181-3. Waterhouse of Halifax.
BRETTON, R. 'The Waterhouse coat of arms', *T.Hal.A.S.* 1942, 11-17.

Wentworth
'Funeral certificates', *Y.A.J.* 12, 1893, 402-4. For Mathew Wentworth, 1637, William Ingleby, 1636, John Louell, 1637, Andrew Agar, 1637, Francis Stringer, 1637, and William Richards, 1637.

Westby
RYLANDS, J. PAUL. 'Arms and crest of John Westby, 1560', *Transactions of the Historic Society of Lancashire and Cheshire* 68; N.S., 32, 1916, 195-8. Of Westby, Yorkshire.

Whitley
BRETTON, ROWLAND. 'Arms of Speaker Whitley', *Coat of arms* 8, 1964-5, 119-21. 20th c.

Wickham
'Armorial bookplate: Wickham', *M.G.H.* N.S., 4, 1884, 67. Of Cottingley, 18-19th c.

Willan
'Grant of arms to James Willan of Kingston upon Hull, 1617', *M.G.H.* 3rd series 1, 1896, 60.

3. DIARIES, LETTERS AND HOUSEHOLD ACCOUNTS

Diaries and letters frequently contain information of value to the genealogist. Many have been published; the list below is selective, and identifies those volumes likely to be of most genealogical interest. Some household accounts are also listed. A number of volumes include several diaries; these are listed first.

WHITING, C.E., ed. *Two Yorkshire diaries: the diary of Arthur Jessop, and Ralph Ward's journal.* Y.A.S., R.S. 117. 1952. These diaries cover 1729-46 and 1754-6 respectively; many names mentioned.

Yorkshire diaries and autobiographies in the seventeenth and eighteenth centuries. Surtees Society 65. 1877. Contents: EYRE, ADAM. 'A dyurnall or catalogue of all my accions and expences from the 1st of January 1646-[7], ed. H.J.Morehouse. 'The life of master John Shaw', ed. Charles Jackson (includes folded pedigree of Shaw, 16-19th c.) FRETWELL, JAMES. 'A family history', ed. Charles Jackson (includes pedigree of Fretwell and Woodhouse, 17-19th c.) HOBSON, JOHN. 'The journal of Mr. John Hobson, late of Dodworth Green', ed. Charles Jackson (includes folded pedigree of Pashley, Fretwell and Hobson, 16-18th c.) DERING, HENEAGE. 'Autobiographical memoranda', ed. Charles Jackson.

Yorkshire diaries & autobiographies in the seventeenth and eighteenth centuries. Surtees Society 77, 1886. Contents: PRIESTLEY, JONATHAN. 'Some memories concerning the family of the Priestleys', ed. Charles Jackson. (written in 1696). 'Memorandum book of Sir Walter Calverley, Bart.', ed. S.Margerison.

Battie
OWEN, F.M. 'Various accounts 1749', *T.Hunter A.S.* 5, 1943, 64-70. Discussion of the account book of William Battie, solicitor, including list of his clients, 1749-74, *etc.* .

Beaumont
MACRAY, W.D. ed. *Beaumont papers: letters relating to the family of Beaumont, of Whitley, Yorkshire, from the fifteenth to the seventeenth centuries.* Roxburgh Club, 1884.

Best
[ROBINSON, C.B.], ed. *Rural economy in Yorkshire in 1641, being the farming and account books of Henry Best of Elmswell in the East Riding of the County of York.* Surtees Society 33. 1857. Includes appendix, 'Elmswell and its owners', with pedigree of Best, 16-18th c., probate records, *etc.*

Bower
POSTLES, DAVID. 'The memoranda book of Samuel Bower,' *Y.A.J.* 56, 1984, 119-29. Includes extracts from a clergyman's memoranda book, with many names; also genealogical notes on Bower.

Clifford
CLIFFORD, D.J.H., ed. *The diaries of Lady Anne Clifford.* Stroud: Alan Sutton, 1990. 17th c., includes pedigree, 13-17th c.
DICKENS, A.G., ed. *Clifford letters of the sixteenth century.* Surtees Society 172. 1962. Includes pedigree, 15-17th c.

Constable
ROEBUCK, PETER, ed. *Constable of Everingham correspondence, 1726-43.* Y.A.S., R.S. 136. 1976.

Dickenson
WIGFULL, JAMES R. 'Extracts from the note-book of William Dickenson', *T.Hunter A.S.* 2(2), 1921, 189-200. 16th c.

Eyre
WESTHAUSER, KARL E. 'Friendship and family in early modern England: the sociability of Adam Eyre and Samuel Pepys', *Journal of social history* 27(3), 1994, 517-36. Based on their diaries.

Grimston
LAUGHTON, J.K. *Report on the manuscripts of Lady Du Cane.* H.M.S.O., 1905. 18th c. letters of the family of Grimston of Grimston Garth and Kilnwick; includes pedigree, medieval-18th c.

Heaton
PAYNE, BRIAN, & PAYNE, DOROTHY, eds. 'Extracts from the diary of John Deakin Heaton, M.D., of Claremont, Leeds', in *Thoresby miscellany* 15. *T.S.* 53. 1973, 93-153. 19th c., includes pedigree.

Heywood

HEYWOOD, OLIVER. *The Rev. Oliver Heywood, B.A., 1630-1702: his autobiography, diaries, anecdote and event books, illustrating the general and family history of Yorkshire and Lancashire.* 4 vols. Brighouse: A.B.Byers, 1882-5. Originally intended to be 3 vols.

Hill

'Extracts from an old Leeds merchant's memorandum book, 1770-1786, and copies of certain loose papers therein', in *Miscellanea* [7]. *T.S.* 24,1919, 31-8. Belonging to Thomas Hill.

Hoby

MEADS, DOROTHY M., ed. *Diary of Lady Margaret Hoby, 1599-1605.* George Routledge & Sons, 1930.

FOX, EVELYN. 'The diary of an Elizabethan gentlewoman', *Transactions of the Royal Historical Society* 3rd series 1, 1908, 153-74. Discussion of the diary of Margaret, Lady Hoby, of Hackness, 1599-1605.

Holden

TOSH, JOHN. 'From Keighley to St.Denis: separation and intimacy in Victorian bourgeois marriage', *History workshop journal* 40, 1995, 193-206. Discussion of Holden family letters.

Jacques

KINGTON, JEAN, ed. 'Diary of a surgeon: extracts from the notebooks of Richard Jacques, surgeon of Grassington', *Wh.N.* 24. 1997, 12-13. 25, 1997, 8-10; 26, 1997, 9-11. Includes notes on the Jacques family, list of babies delivered, 1813-28, *etc.*

Johnson

GUNNELL, W.A. *Sketches of Hull celebrities, or, memoirs and correspondence of Thomas Johnson and four of his lineal descendants from 1640 to 1858.* Hull: Walker & Brown, 1876. Includes many brief biographies.

Lister, Anne

GREEN, MURIEL M., ed. *Miss Lister of Shibden Hall: selected letters (1800-1840).* Lewes: Book Guild, 1992.

LIDDINGTON, JILL. 'Anne Lister and Shibden Hall, Halifax (1791-1840): re-reading the correspondence', *T.Hal.A.S.* N.S., 1, 1993, 62-78.

LIDDINGTON, JILL. 'Anne Lister of Shibden Hall, Halifax, (1791-1840): her diaries and the historians', *History workshop: a journal of socialist and feminist historians* 35, 1993, 45-77. Discussion of the diaries and how they have been used.

WHITBREAD, HELENA, ed. *I know my own heart: the diaries of Anne Lister 1791-1840.* New York: New York University Press, 1992.

WHITBREAD, HELENA, ed. *No priest but love: excerpts from the diary of Anne Lister, 1824-1826.* Otley: Smith Settle, 1992.

Lister, Septimus

LISTER, SEPTIMUS. *An old Ecclesfield diary,* ed. Thomas Winder. Sheffield: J.W, Northend, 1921. Includes many notices of births, marriages and deaths, 18-19th c.

LOCKWOOD, WILLIAM. *Ye dear object of my affections: the diary of William Lockwood of Easingwold, 1778-1836, from 1st January 1796 to 30th September 1797, including a tour of the Lake District, and a record of his income and expenditure for the years 1797 and 1798,* ed. Helen Kirk. Easingwold: Forest of Galtres Society, 1996. Includes pedigree, 18-20th c., and notes on persons named.

Lonsdale

PLAYNE, ELIZABETH, & BOER, G. DE., ed. *Lonsdale documents.* Surtees Society 188. 1973. Letters of Rev. John Lonsdale, of Masham, early 19th c. Includes pedigree of Lonsdale, 18-20th c.

Maude

BAILDON, W.PALEY. 'Some correspondence of the Maudes of Hollinghall, 1594-1599', in *Miscellanea* [7]. *T.S.* 24, 1919, 110-33.

Peckitt

BRIGHTON, J.T. 'William Peckitt's commission book 1751-1795', *Walpole Society* 54, 1991 for 1988, 334-453. Transcript, listing the commissions received by a glass painter of York; includes biographical notes on patrons.

Percy

BATHO, G.R., ed. *The household papers of Henry Percy, ninth Earl of Northumberland, 1564-1632.* Camden 3rd series **93**. Royal Historical Society, 1962. The nucleus of the Earl's estate lay in Yorkshire.

Pickering

LUMB, G.D. 'Justice's note-book of Captain John Pickering, 1656-1660', in *Miscellanea* **[4]**. *T.S.* **11**, 1904, 69-100; *Miscellanea* **[5]**. *T.S.* **15**, 1909, 71-80 & 277-95. Includes some marriages, as well as much else.

Plaxton

WALKER, E.M. 'Letters of the Rev. George Plaxton, M.A.', *Thoresby Miscellany* **11**. *T.S.* **37**. 1936, 30-104. 1706-9., includes brief notes on persons mentioned.

Plumpton

KIRBY, JOAN, ed. *The Plumpton letters and papers.* Camden 5th series **8**. 1996. Includes Plumpton pedigree, 14-17th c., with biographical notes on persons mentioned.

STAPLETON, THOMAS, ed. *Plumpton correspondence: a series of letters, chiefly domestick, written in the reigns of Edward IV, Richard III, Henry VII and Henry VIII edited from Sir Edward Plumpton's book of letters, with notices historical and biographical of the family of Plumpton, Co. Ebor.* Camden Society old series **4**. 1839. Includes folded pedigree of Plumpton, 15-17th c., also pedigree of Foljambe of Hassop, Derbyshire, 14th c.

TAYLOR, J. 'The Plumpton letters 1416-1552', *N.H.* **10**, 1975, 72-87.

Pryme

JACKSON, CHARLES, ed. *The diary of Abraham de la Pryme, the Yorkshire antiquary.* Surtees Society **54**. 1869. Includes folded pedigree of De La Pryme, 17-19th c., also much information on the county's heritage.

Sharp

CROWTHER, JANICE E., & CROWTHER, PETER A., ed. *The diary of Robert Sharp of South Cave: life in a Yorkshire village, 1812-1837.* Records of social and economic history N.S. **26**. Oxford: Oxford University Press for the British Academy, 1997. Includes 'brief biographies of local people in the diary'; also pedigree of Sharp, 18-20th c.

Simpson

SIMPSON, JOHN. *The journal of Dr. John Simpson of Bradford, 1825.* Bradford: Bradford Metropolitan Council Libraries Division, Local Studies Department, 1981.

Slingsby

SLINGSBY, HENRY, SIR. *The diary of Sir Henry Slingsby of Scriven, Bart., ...* Longman, Rees, Orme, Brown and Green, 1836. Covers 1638-46; includes a genealogical memoir.

Stapleton

COX, J. CHARLES. 'The household book of Sir Miles Stapleton, Bart., 1656-1705', *Ancestor* **2**, 1902, 17-39; **3**, 1902, 132-62.

Tate

WENHAM, L.P., ed. *Letters of James Tate.* Y.A.S., R.S. **128**. 1966. 1791-1818.

Thoresby

THORESBY, RALPH. *The diary of Ralph Thoresby, F.R.S., author of the Topography of Leeds (1677-1724).* ed. Joseph Hunter. 2 vols. Henry Colburn and Richard Bentley, 1830.

LANCASTER, W.T., ed. *Letters addressed to Ralph Thoresby, F.R.S., printed from the originals in the possession of the Yorkshire Archaeological Society.* T.S. **21**. 1912.

Letters of eminent men addressed to Ralph Thoresby, F.R.S. 2 vols. Henry Colburn, 1832.

HARGRAVE, EMILY. 'Some hitherto unpublished letters of Ralph Thoresby', in *Miscellanea* **[8]**. *T.S.* **26**, 1924, 372-96.

Turner

LAW, EDWARD J. *18th century Huddersfield: the day-books of John Turner, 1732-1773.* Huddersfield: Edmund. J. Law, 1985. Records of an attorney; includes many notes on births and deaths, and numerous other names.

Weatherill

DIXON, GRACE. 'The diary of Anne Weatherill', *C.T.L.H.S.B.* **53**, 1987, 11-19. Includes pedigree, 19th c.

Worsley

HAWKESBURY, LORD. 'The ms. Account and memorandum book of a lady of a Yorkshire lady two centuries ago', *T.E.R.A.S.* **9**, 1902, 1-56. Household accounts of Mary Worsley, 1696-1724, with pedigrees of Fairfax, Foljambe, Gower, Savile, Aske, White, Wentworth, *etc.*

4. SURNAMES.

The study of surname origins and distribution is a fascinating subject in its own right, and has obvious relevance for genealogists. For studies of particular surnames see section 6 below. The authoritative general survey for the West Riding is:

REDMONDS, GEORGE. *Yorkshire West Riding.* English surnames series 1. Phillimore & Co., 1973.

See also:

DYSON, TAYLOR. *Place names and surnames, their origin and meaning, with special reference to the West Riding of Yorkshire.* Huddersfield: Alfred Jubb & Son, 1944.

JENSEN, GILLIAN FELLOWS. *Scandinavian personal names in Lincolnshire and Yorkshire.* Copenhagen: Ikommission hos Akademisk forlag, 1968.

ROGERS, K.A. *Vikings & surnames,* York: William Sessions, 1991. General study of surnames found in the York and district telephone directory for 1979.

ROGERS, K.H. *More Vikings and surnames.* Barnsley: Kings England Press, 1995. Not seen.

Aldborough

LAWSON-TANCRED, THOMAS, SIR. 'Old parish surnames at Aldborough', *Y.A.J.* **31**, 1934, 65-73. Lists surnames, 14-15th c.

Bradford

REDMONDS, GEORGE. *Yorkshire surnames series, part 1: Bradford & District.* The author, 1990.

Cleveland

ATKINSON, J.C. 'Some notes on personal names obtaining in Cleveland in 1302', *Reliquary* N.S., **4**, 1890, 201-7.

ATKINSON, J.C. 'Further remarks on personal names and their distribution in 1302', *Reliquary* **5**, 1891, 84-9.

Halifax

SENIOR, A. 'Local place-names and surnames', *T.Hal.A.S.* 1951, 15-35. Based on the 1379 lay subsidy for Halifax.

Nidderdale

TURNER, MAURICE. 'Distribution and persistence of surnames in a Yorkshire dale, 1500-1750', *Local population studies* **54**, 1995, 28-39. Nidderdale; based on tax lists and parish registers.

Pickering

RIMINGTON, F.C. 'Local surnames of the middle ages', *Scarborough and District Archaeological Society transactions* **1**(5), 1962, 15-17. In the records of the Honor and Forest of Pickering.

Saddleworth

'Saddleworth forenames in the seventeenth and eighteenth centuries', *B.S.H.S.* **23**(3), 1993, 1-6. Includes list of common names from parish register.

Sheffield

HEY, DAVID, ed. *The origins of one hundred Sheffield surnames.* Sheffield: University of Sheffield Division of Adult Continuing Education, 1992.

5. BIOGRAPHICAL DICTIONARIES

Quite a number of Yorkshire biographical dictionaries are available, although most of the county-wide volumes provide contemporary biographies only. Historical dictionaries include:

COLBECK, MAURICE. *Yorkshire history makers.* Wakefield: EP Publishing, 1976. 12 brief biographies of prominent Yorkshire men.

COLERIDGE, HARTLEY. *Lives of northern worthies,* ed. D. Coleridge. New ed. 3 vols. E. Moxon, 1852. Previous editions published as *Biographia borealis* (1833), and *The Worthies of Yorkshire and Lancashire* (1836). Biographies of 12 prominent 'worthies'.

HARTLEY, MARIE, & INGLEBY, JOAN. *Yorkshire portraits.* J.M.Dent & Sons, 1961. Brief biographies.

HEALD, BOWMAN. 'Eminent Yorkshiremen', *Y.N.Q.II* **5**, 1909, 244-51. Brief biographical dictionary of over 200 indivudals.

CLAY, J.W. 'The gentry of Yorkshire at the time of the Civil War', *Y.A.J.* **23**, 1915, 349-94. Biographical dictionary of Royalists and Parliamentarians.

Contemporary biographical dictionaries are listed in date order.

1892

PRESS, C.A.MANNING. *Yorkshire leaders, social and political.* 2 vols. Leeds: McCorquodale & Co., 1892.

1898

Yorkshire men of mark. Exeter: William Pollard & Co., 1898, Reproduced on 2 fiche in the *British and Irish biographies* collection, Cambridge: Chadwyck-Healey, 1990. Brief current biographies.

1899

Yorkshire lives social and political. Gaskill Jones & Co., 1899. Brief current biographies.

1902

SCOTT, W. HERBERT. *The West Riding of Yorkshire at the opening of the twentieth century.* Pike's new century series **6**. Brighton: W.T. Pike & Co., 1902. Includes *Contemporary biographies*, ed. W.T. Pike, reprinted in facsimile as: SCOTT, W.H., & PIKE, W.T. *A dictionary of Edwardian biography: West Riding of Yorkshire.* Edinburgh: Peter Bell, 1987.

1903

SCOTT, W. HERBERT. *The North and East Ridings of Yorkshire at the opening of the twentieth century.* Pike's new century series **8**. Brighton: W.T. Pike & Co., 1903. Includes *Contemporary biographies*, ed. W.T. Pike, which is reprinted in facsimile in: SCOTT, W.H., & PIKE, W.T. *A dictionary of Edwardian biography: Yorkshire, North and East Ridings.* Edinburgh: Peter Bell, 1987.

1908

PRESS, C.A.MANNING. *Yorkshire leaders: social and political.* Queenhithe Printing & Publishing Co., 1908. Reproduced on 3 fiche in the *British and Irish biographies 1840-1940* collection, Cambridge: Chadwyck-Healey, 1996.

1912

Yorkshire who's who. Westminster Publishing Co., 1912.

1935

Who's who in Yorkshire (North and East Ridings). Hereford: Jakeman & Co., 1935.

Barnsley

WILKINSON, JOSEPH. *Worthies, families and celebrities of Barnsley and the district.* Bemrose & Sons, [1883]. Histories of twelve families.

East Riding

HAWKESBURY, LORD. 'Some East Riding families', *T.E.R.A.S.* **7**, 1899, 1-36. Brief notes on lesser gentry families, alphabetical.

Halifax

TURNER, J. HORSFALL. *Biographia Halifaxiensis, or, Halifax families and worthies: a biographical and genealogical history of Halifax parish.* Bingley: T. Harrison, 1883.

Leeds

TAYLOR, R. V. *The biographia Leodiensis, or, biographical sketches of the worthies of Leeds and neighbourhood, from the Norman Conquest to the present time.* Simpkin Marshall & Co., 1865. Supplement 1867.

MORKILL, J.W. 'Local worthies and genealogy', in *Miscellanea* **1**. *T.S.* **2**. 1891, 51-4. Includes folded pedigrees, *etc.,* of Falshaw of Leeds, 18-19th c., Smeaton of Austhorpe Lodge, 18th c., Graveley of Hatton 17-19th c.,

Pudsey

RAYNER, SIMEON. 'Eminent townsmen of Pudsey', *B.A.* **1**, 1888, 33-44. Brief biographical notes.

Sheffield

'Big and little guns of Sheffield', *N.& Q.* 1(2), 1899, 119-43; 1(3), 1899, 191-215; 1(4), 1899, 261-85; 2(1), 1900, 47-71; 2(2), 1900, 119-43; 2(3), 1900, 191-215; 2(4), 1900, 261-85. Brief biographies of contemporary notables.

Sheffield at the opening of the 20th century: contemporary biographies. Pikes new century series **4**. Brighton: W.T. Pike, 1901. The biographical portion is reprinted in facsimile in: ODDY, S.O., & PIKE, W.T. *A dictionary of Edwardian biography: Sheffield and neighbourhood.* Edinburgh: Peter Bell, 1987.

ODOM, W. *Hallamshire worthies: characteristics and work of notable Sheffield men and woman.* Sheffield: J.W. Northend, 1926.

Sheffield and District who's who. Sheffield: Sir W.C.Leng & Co., 1905.

Wakefield

CAMERON, JOHN. *The notabilities of Wakefield and its neighbourhood.* Sherwood Gilbert and Piper, 1843. Eight biographies.

LUPTON, J.H. *Wakefield worthies, or, biographical sketches of men of note connected by birth, or otherwise, with the town of Wakefield in Yorkshire.* Hamilton & Co., 1864.

Warley

SUTCLIFFE, TOM. 'Warley worthies', *P.R.H.A.S.* 1916, 73-111. Brief biographies.

Portraits

A number of works listing portraits are available; some of them include biographical and genealogical notes on the individuals portrayed. Consult:

HAILSTONE, EDWARD, ed. *Portraits of Yorkshire worthies, selected from the national exhibition of works of art at Leeds, 1868.* 2 vols. Cundall and Fleming, 1869. Includes brief biographies of persons portrayed, with portraits.

HAWKESBURY, LORD. 'Catalogue of the portraits, miniatures, &c., at Castle Howard', *T.E.R.A.S.* 11, 1903, 35-86. Extensive list.

HAWKESBURY, LORD. 'East Riding portraits', *T.E.R.A.S.* 10, 1903, 27-69. List of portraits in various collections.

'Catalogue of portraits, miniatures &c., at Kirkham Abbey in the possession of Lord Hawkesbury', *T.E.R.A.S.* 13(1), 1906, 1-139. Also at Lord Hawkesbury's London house; includes many plates, and biographical notes on persons portrayed, with folded pedigree showing relationships of innumerable families.

6. FAMILY HISTORIES AND PEDIGREES

A(c)kroyd

BROWN, COLIN M. 'Copley School and the Akroyd family', *T.Hal.A.S.* 1984, 59-66. 19th c.

REDMONDS, GEORGE. 'The origins of Yorkshire 'Royd' surnames', *O.W.R.* 1(1), 1981, 30-35. Brief notes on Ackroyd, Boothroyd, Buckroyd, Greenroyd, Holroyd, Learoyde, Murgatroyd, Oldroyd, Ormondroyd, Royde, Stainrod, *etc.*

See also Smith

Adamson

'More about the Adamson family bible', *B.T.* 46, 1991, 7. See also 42, 1990, 26-7. 19-20th c.

Addy

ADDY, S.O. 'The Addy family of Darton and elsewhere in the West Riding', *Y.A.J.* 27, 1924, 166-86. Includes pedigrees, 16-19th c.

Adkins

HINCHLIFFE, G. 'The home of the Adkins, cricketing plumbers', *Newsletter / Y.A.S. Local History Study Section* 29, 1988, 10-12. 19th c.

Ainsley

AINSLEY, W.C. 'An old Bilsdale family', *Ryedale historian* 15, 1990-91, 12-15. Ainsley family, 18-20th c.

MITCHELL, JOYCE. 'The Ainsley House', *J.Cl.F.H.S.* 7(1), 1998, 42-5. Ainsley family of Stokesley, Hartlepool, *etc.,* 19th c.

Ainsworth

BEATTIE, NEIL. 'The Ainsworth family: links with Saddleworth', *B.S.H.S.* 28(1), 1998, 6-8. 18th c.

Aislabie

NORRIS, KIT. 'The Aislabie family of Studley Royal', *R.H.* 4(1) 1999, 22-4. 17-18th c.

SCATTERGOOD, BERNARD P. 'The Aislaby family of Studley', *Notes and queries* 164, 1933, 318. See also 358. Brief note, 18th c.

WALBRAN, JOHN RICHARD. *A genealogical memoir of the lords of Studley in Yorkshire.* Ripon: William Harrison, 1841. Aislabie family, 12-18th c. Scarce; reprinted in: WALBRAN, J.R., & RAINE, JAMES, junior, eds. *Memorials of the abbey of St. Mary of Fountains ... vol.II, part 1.* Surtees Society **67**. 1878.

Akrigg

AKRIGG, G.P.V. *The name of Akrigg ...* Vancouver: Privately printed, 1964. Originally of the Sedbergh area. Brief pamphlet.

Akroyd

See A(c)kroyd

Aldeburgh

DUCKETT, GEORGE, SIR. 'Family of Aldeburgh: Harwood evidences', *Y.A.J.* **4**, 1877, 96-107. Includes medieval pedigree.

Alderson

DEAN, JOHN. 'Guest society: the Alderson Family History Society', *Family tree magazine* **13**(12), 1997, 5.

Aldham

See Smith

Aldred

ALDRED, HENRY. 'The family of Aldred', *Old Yorkshire* **8**, 1891, 190-94. 18-19th c.

Alexander

BRETTON, R. 'Alexanders of Halifax', *T.Hal.A.S.* 1947, 27-53. 18-20th c.

Alford

'Alford', *M.G.H.* 2nd series **1**, 1886, 208-9. Undated pedigree; of Derbyshire, Hertfordshire, Yorkshire, *etc.*

Allcard

PLATTS, MARGARET. 'The Allcards and their occupations', *F.S.* **10** (2), 1989, 44-8. Of Bakewell, Sheffield, *etc.,* 18-20th c.

Alost

See Constable

Alured

PINK, WM. DUNCOMBE. 'Alured of Charterhouse, Co. York', *Y.G.* **1**, 1888, 1-12. 16-18th c., includes wills and pedigree.

Ambler

PINDER, JANE. 'The Ambler family, part four: back to our roots', *K.D.F.H.S.J.* Winter 1997, 8-9. 18-19th c.

PINDER, JANE. 'Have you ever thought of writing a chronology?' *K.D.F.H.S.J.* Winter 1996, 21-2. Includes chronology of Ambler family, 19th c.

'Pedigree of Ambler', *K.D.F.H.S.J.* Summer 1994, 14-15. 18-20th c.

'Pedigree of Ambler', *K.D.F.H.S.J.* Autumn 1995, 14-15. 19-20th c.

Andrew

GILLOT, HEATHER. 'The Andrew family and the Earl Grey', *F.S.* **11**(1), 1990, 21-2. 19th c., the Earl Grey was a Sheffield pub.

Anelay

STAPLETON, H.E.C. ed. *A skilful master-builder: the continuing story of a Yorkshire family business, craftsmen for seven generations.* William Anelay, 1975. Anelay family, includes pedigree, 17-19th c.

Anne

ANNE, E.M. CHARLTON. *Burghwallis and the Anne family.* Burghwallis: St. Annes Convent, 1968. Medieval-19th c.

Appleton

APPLETON, KELVIN. 'The Appletons of Goodmanham and the Stephensons of Arras', *B.T.* **49**, 1992, 27-8. 17-19th c.

Appleyard

ALDRED, HENRY W. 'Appleyard family,' *Y.G.* **1**, 1888, 118-38. Medieval-19th c.
See also Leverthorpe

Armitage / Armytage

ARMYTAGE, G.J. 'Armytage of Kerresforth Hill', *M.G.H.* N.S., **1**, 1874, 436-41. Includes pedigree, extracts from Barnsley parish register, monumental inscriptions, and wills, 15-17th c.

AXON, ERNEST. 'Armytage of Lightcliffe', *Y.G.* **2**, 1890, 27-8. Includes pedigree, 18-19th c.

I'ANSON, ARTHUR B. *The history of the Armytage or Armitage family.* Hazell Watson and Viney, [1915]. Of Lancashire and Yorkshire, *etc.,* medieval-20th c.

'Armitage family', *M.G.H.* N.S., **3**, 1880, 99-123. 13-15th c.

'Armytage of Kirklees', *M.G.H.* **2**, 1876, 87-94. Pedigrees, 17-18th c., extracts from parish registers of York, Hartshead, and South Kirkby; will abstracts, *etc.*

'Armytage of Netherton', *M.G.H.* **2**, 1876, 179-80. Extracts from Thornhill parish registers, with pedigree, 17-18th c.

The pedigree of the Armitage family, reprinted from an ancient book. Mitre Press, [1931]. 17-18th c., includes extracts from Barnsley parish registers.

See also Coltman, Green and Hassard

Arthington

BARRITT, M. 'Calling any Arthingtons of Yorkshire', *Y.F.H.* **16**(4), 1990, 100-101. Includes pedigree, 18-19th c.

Arundel

NORSWORTHY, L.L. 'The Yorkshire Arundels', *Notes & queries* **193**, 1948, 24-6, 93-5, 183-5, 221-4, 332-5, 380-82, & 488-91; **194**, 1949, 55-60. 12-19th c.

Ashworth

See Roberson

Aske

ELLIS, A.S. 'Notes on some East Riding families and their arms', *T.E.R.A.S.* **6**, 1898, 43-55. On the Askes of Aughton, and the De Araines, medieval.

HUNTLEY, LOCKWOOD. *The Askes of Aske Hall and of Aughton.* Historic Yorkshire families series **10**. York: North of England Newspaper Co., 1905. Reprinted from the *Yorkshire gazette.*

SALTMARSHE, PHILIP. 'The Aske family', *T.E.R.A.S.* **17**, 1910, 1-22. 16-17th c.

Aspinall

REDMONDS, G. 'Lancashire surnames in Yorkshire: the distribution and development of Aspinall and Ridehalgh in the West Riding', *Genealogists' magazine* **18**(1), 1975, 13-18.

Atkinson

ATKINSON, F. 'Enigma variations on the Atkinsons of Woodhouse', *C.Y.D.F.H.S.J.* **43**, 1999, 22-3. 18-19th c.

ATKINSON, HAROLD WARING. *The families of Atkinson of Roxby (Lincs) and Thorne, and Dearman of Braithwaite, and families connected with them, especially Atkinson-Busfeild, Barnes, Beavington, Birchall, Edwards, Miller, Neave, Ransome, Rooke, Sessions, Sinclair, Somerford, Stanley, Waring, Wykeham.* Northwood, Middlesex: the author, 1933. Includes extracts from wills and many other records.

Audley

'Audley of Patrington-in-Holderness, co. York', in READE, ALEYN LYELL. *The Audley pedigrees.* Percy Lund Humphries and Co., 1929, Pt. 1, 85-8.

Awmack

AWMACK, JOSEPH. 'The Awmacks of Borrowby', *Y.F.H.S.N.* **13**, 1986, 16-19; **14**, 1986, 24-5. Includes pedigree, 18-19th c.

AWMACK, J.W. 'The Awmacks of Harome', *Ryedale historian* **15**, 1990-91, 20-21. Includes pedigrees, 16-19th c.

Aykroyd

DE COSTOBADIE, F. PALLISER. *History of the family of Aykroyd of Aykroyd in the County of York, A.D. 1381-1933 ...* Privately printed, 1934.

Ayrton

See Craven

Backhouse

BACKHOUSE, JAMES. *Select family memoirs.* York: William Alexander & Co., 1831. Of Lancashire, Darlington and Yorkshire, *etc.,* 17-19th c.

Backus

BINGHAM, EVERETT F. 'William Backus of Sheffield, Yorkshire, and Norwich, Connecticut', *New England historical and genealogical register* **142**, 1988, 253-4. See also **143**, 1989, 24. 17th c.

Bagshawe

HIMSWORTH, J.B. 'Some notes on the provenance of the Bagshawe family of Derbyshire and Sheffield', *T.Hunter A.S.* **7**, 1957, 277. Brief notes.

Baildon

BAILDON, WILLIAM PALEY. *Baildon and the Baildons: a history of a Yorkshire manor and family.* 3 vols. St Catherine Press, 1913-27. Vol. 1 is devoted to the manor, and gives accounts of various different families; vols. 2-3 are devoted to the Baildon family, and include numerous pedigrees. Extensive.

BAILDON, W. PALEY. 'A rectors letters, 1', *Ancestor* 1, 1902, 160-65. Baildon family, 16-17th c.

Bainbridge

'An attempt to trace the English ancestry of Commodore Bainbridge', *New England historical and genealogical register* 22, 1868, 18-20. Includes medieval pedigree.

Bairstow

TRIGG, W.B. 'Brownhirst and the Bairstows', *P.R.H.A.S.* 1926, 101-28. 15-18th c. In Ovenden Wood.

Baldwin

BALDWIN, HUGH. *Annals of my ancestors.* Exeter: privately published, 1935. Baldwin family, 15-19th c.

BALDWIN, J.R. *Some account of the Baldwins of Ingthorpe Grange, Craven, Yorks.* Leamington Spa: Frank Glover, 1905. Includes pedigree, 15-19th c.

Baliol

MORIARTY, G. ANDREWS. 'The Baliols in Picardy, England, and Scotland, *New England historical and genealogical register* 106, 1952, 273-90. Medieval; the family held the baronies of Bywell and Barnard Castle and the Yorkshire Honour of Stokesley, *etc.*

Ballan

'My great-great-great-uncle was a Mormon', *C.Y.D.F.H.S.J.* 27, 1992, 24-5. Ballan family, of York and Salt Lake City 19th c.

Balme

'The Balmes of Bradford and Birstall', *Y.G.* 1, 1888, 16-19. 16-17th c. Not completed.

Baltimore

See Calvert

Banks

See Tupholme

Barber

WILLIAMS, T.J. 'Notes on the Barber family of Castle Hill, Rastrick', *T.Hal.A.S.* 49-56. 19th c.

'Historical memoranda of the enquiry of the Barber's pedigree and cause thereof', *R.H.* 2(7), 1994, 172-5. Barber family, 18th c.

Barker

BROWN, D.M. 'Frustrations', *F.S.* 18(3), 1997, 87-91. Barker family of Norton, Eckington, Handsworth, *etc.,* 19-20th c.

Barnes

See Atkinson

Barnett

GIBBS, H.H. 'Fly-leaves of Archbishop Sharpe's sermons, 1701, belonging to Eleanora Barnett, afterwards Eleanora Hucks', *M.G.H.* N.S., 3, 1880, 265. Memoranda relating to the Barnett family of Knaresborough, 18th c.

Baron

APPLEBY, JOHN. 'My search for Anne Baron', *Y.A.S., F.H.P.S.S.N.* 5(5), 1979, 78-9. 19th c.

Barraclough

BENNETT, STEPHEN L.G 'Auntie Pollie's little red book', *Y.F.H.* 15(1), 1989, 24-6. Notes on Barraclough, Newsome and Bingley families, 19th c.

Barras

'Family tree of Mary Barras', *Cameo* 1992, no. 3, 10. Otherwise Barrowes or Burrows; 17-19th c.

Barrowclough

REDMONDS, GEORGE. 'Surname history: Barrowclough', *H. & D.F.H.S.J.* 8(2), 1995, 71.

Barrowes

See Barras

Bartlett

SCRUTON, WILLIAM. 'The Bartlett family', *B.A.* 1, 1888, 187-91. 17-18th c.

Barton
STEDMAN, JOHN. *Memoir of the family of Barton, of Barton, Fryton and Oswaldkirk in the County of York, continued through that of Mowbray of Barnbougle in the County of Edinburgh and that of Stedman, of Little Steggie, Kinross, and Ballingall in the County of Kinross.* Bath: Hallway and Son, 1857. Medieval-19th c.
See also Smith

Barwick
ALBERTI, C.F. 'Pedigree of Barwick', *K.D.F.H.S.J.* Winter 1998, 14-15. 19-20th c.

Bashforth
BASHFORTH, T.S. 'Bashforth', *F.S.* 1 (3), 1978, 68-9. One-name study.

Batchelor
BATCHELOR, ANNE. 'A flower for Theophilus', *Y.F.H.* 14(6), 1988, 131-6. Batchelor family of Buckinghamshire, Hertfordshire and Yorkshire, 16-19th c.

Bates
BATES, J.C. 'The Bates family of Ovenden', *T.Hal.A.S.* 1982, 38-60. Medieval-18th c.

Bathurst
'Rainwater hoods and fallpipe brackets, part IV', *Y.A.S., F.H.P.S.S.N.* 5(4), 1979, 57-8. Bathurst family, includes pedigree, 17-18th c.

Battye
REDMONDS, GEORGE. 'Surname history: Battye', *H.D.F.H.S.J.* 1(2) 1988, 43.

Bayeux
See Bayne

Baxter
KAPP, ELEANOR. 'Eleanor Baxter's journey', *Y.F.H.* 12(2), 1986, 34-6. Includes pedigree showing connection to Simpson, 17-18th c.

Bayley
See Peirse

Bayne
LUCAS, JOSEPH. *Historical genealogy of the family of Bayne of Nidderdale, showing also how Bayeux became Bayne.* Ripon: William Harrison, 1896. Includes extracts from 144 deeds, 16 pedigrees, various wills, *etc., etc.*

Beadle
FENWICK-BEADLE, KEITH ROBERT MAIN. *Beadle: a branch of a Holderness family.* Hull: [the author?] 1980. Pamphlet.

Bearpark
BEARPARK, MICHAEL. 'The Bearpark name in the North-East', *C.Y.D.F.H.S.J.* **26**, 1992, 31. General discussion.

Beaumont
BEAUMONT, THOMAS. 'The unremarkable Beaumonts of Darton', *O.W.R.* 4(1), 1984, 14-15. 18th c.

Beavington
See Atkinson

Beckwith
'Entries respecting the Beckwith family in a black letter bible ...', *M.G.H.* 2nd series **4**, 1892, 155-6. Of Rothwell, 18th c.

Bedford
BEDFORD, EDWIN JACKSON. 'Pedigree of the Bedfords of Hull, Dewsbury, Penistone, *etc.,* Co. York', *M.G.H.* N.S., **3**. 1880, 189-93. See also 332-3. 15-19th c.
'Pedigree of Bedford of Oughtibridge, in the chapelry of Bradfield, Co. York, descended from Grayson and Hull', *M.G.H.* N.S., **4**, 1884, 197-8. 16-19th c.
See also Rawlins

Beeston
LANCASTER, W.T. 'The family of Beeston', in *Miscellanea* **[6]**. *T.S.* **24**, 1919, 245-55. Medieval-18th c.
'Pedigree of the very ancient family of Beestons of Beeston', *Genealogist* **1**, 1877, 175-6. 13-16th c.

Beetham
MACRAE, JOHN. 'The Beetham family', *Don. Anc.* 2(2), 1983, 41-4; 2(3), 1984, 87-92. 17-19th c.

Beevor
CARTER, ANNE. *The Beevor story.* Norwich: the author, 1993. 17-20th c. Originally of Penistone, subsequently of Norfolk. Includes pedigrees.

Belasyse

SMITH, GEOFFREY RIDSDILL. *In well beware: the story of Newburgh Priory and the Belasyse family, 1145-1977.* Kineton: Roundwood Press, 1978.

Bell

WAGNER, ANTHONY. 'Papers of a middling family: Bell of Belford, Hull, and Henley in Arden', in EMMISON, FREDERICK, & STEPHENS, ROY, eds. *Tribute to an antiquary: essays presented to Marc Fitch by some of his friends.* Leopards Head Press, 1976, 265-304. Includes pedigree, 17-20th c., and various letters, *etc.*

Belwood

LOW, JILL. 'William Belwood: architect and surveyor', *Y.A.J.* **56**, 1984, 131-54. Includes pedigree, 17-18th c.

Bennett

FREEMANTLE, W.T. *Sterndale Bennett and Sheffield, comprising an account of the Bennett family - Derbyshire, Cambridge and Sheffield. Part I. Also, part II. Sir William Sterndale Bennett and associations with his native city.* Sheffield: Pawson and Brialsford, 1919. 18th c.
See also Whitaker

Benson

BENSON, ARTHUR CHRISTOPHER. *Genealogy of the family of Benson of Banger House and Northwoods, in the parish of Ripon & chapelry of Pateley Bridge.* Eton: George New, 1895. Includes folded pedigrees of Benson, 14-19th c., also of Sidgwick of Stonegappe and Skipton Castle, 18-19th c., of Smith of Halifax and Bingley, 18-19th c., and of Hodgson of High Cayton and Nunwick, 18-19th c.
GORDON-SMITH, R. 'Benson and Smith families', *Notes & queries* 12th series **10**, 1922, 387-8. Of Leeds, *etc.,* 18-19th c.
GORDON-SMITH, R. 'The Rev. Joseph Benson and the *D.N.B.*', *Notes & queries* 12th series **9**, 1921, 327-8. Of Yorkshire and City Road, London, *etc.,* includes notes on family, 18-19th c.
'Bensons from Knaresbro' parish register', *Y.C.M.* **2**, 1892, 231-4. 1565-1700.

'[Benson pedigree]', *Y.C.M.* **3**, 1993 35-7. 16-18th c.
WILLIAMS, DAVID. *Genesis and exodus: a portrait of the Benson family.* Hamish Hamilton, 1979. Includes pedigree, 18-19th c.

Bentley

CUDWORTH, WM. 'Old Bradford lawyers: the Bentley family', *B.A.* **2**, 1895, 65-71. Includes pedigree, 18-19th c.

Best

FLETCHER, W.G. DIMOCK. 'Pedigree of Best, of Perry Hall, Co. Stafford, from Yorkshire', *M.G.H.* N.S., **4**, 1884, 202. 17th c.
LAWRANCE, H. 'Optimus est qui optime facit: a chapter in the family of Best of Elmswell', *T.E.R.A.S.* **11**, 1903, 31-4. Mainly 18-19th c.

Beswick
See Royd(s)

Bethell

PINK, W.D. 'Bethell', *Y.G.* **2**, 1890, 42-4. 17th c.

Billam

BYLLAM-BARNES, PETER. 'Francis Billam, surgeon', *Y.F.H.* **23**(3), 1997, 69-70. Billam family, 18th c.

Bingley
See Barraclough

Birchall
See Atkinson

Blackburn(e)

BANKS, N. 'John Blackburn of Burghwallis', *Y.F.H.* **19**(5), 1993, 109-11. 19th c.
POYNTON, FRANCIS JOHN. *Genealogical memoranda relating to the family of Blackburne and its alliances.* Mitchell & Hughes, 1874. Pedigree, 17-19th c.
'Table shewing the pedigree of Blackburne of Richmond, Grinton, and Marrick in the County of York, with collateral descents of Wilson of Eshton, Malham of Elslack, Poynton, Frend and others', *M.G.H.* N.S., **1**, 1877 77-9. See also 585-6. 17-19th c.

Blacker

WALKER, J.W. 'The Blackers of Blacker, near Worsborough and Crigglestone, in the West Riding of the County of York, 1250-1650', *Y.A.J.* **35**, 1943, 235-60. Includes pedigree, 13-17th c.

Blackett

S[TRAKER], JOHN. *Memoirs of the public life of Sir Walter Blackett, of Wallington, Baronet, with a pedigree of the Calverleys, of Calverley in Yorkshire, and the Blacketts of Newcastle upon Tyne and Northumberland.* Newcastle: S. Hodgson, 1819. 18-19th c. Wallington is in Northumberland.

Blake

RAINE, JAMES. 'Notices of Scoreby and of the family of Blake', *Y.A.J.* **10**, 1889, 83-103. 16th c.
See also Skeet

Blakiston

BLAKISTON, HERBERT E.D. *The family of Blakiston of Stapleton-on-Tees.* Oxford: Oxford University Press, 1928. Includes folded pedigree, 16-19th c.
See also Whitaker

Blanchard

FOX, J. 'Blanchard, stone mason', *J.Cl.F.H.S.* **5**(9), 1994, 18-22. Of Topcliffe, 18th c.

Bland

BLAND, J. 'Pedigree of Bland', *K.D.F.H.S.J.* Autumn 1998, 14-15. 18-20th c.
CARLISLE, N. *Collections for a history of the ancient family of Bland.* W. Nichol, 1826. Of Yorkshire, London and various other counties, 11-19th c. Includes many pedigrees.
'Blands of Halifax', *Y.G.* **1**, 1888, 187-9. Pedigree, 18-19th c.

Bolling

EMPSALL, T.T. 'The Bolling family', *B.A.* **2**, 1895, 117-26 & 173-80. 15-19th c.
TEMPEST, ELEANOR BLANCHE. 'Notes on the early Bollings of Bolling', *B.A.* **6**; N.S., **4**. 1921, 215-34. Medieval.

Booth

POTTS, JOHN D. 'An heriditary gamekeeper (1769-1853)', *F.S.* **6** (1), 1985, 23-5. Booth of Thornton le Dale.
See also Walker

Boothroyd
See Ackroyd

Bosvil(l)e

MACDONALD, ALICE BOSVILLE. *The fortunes of a family (Bosville of New Hall, Gunthwaite and Thorpe) through nine centuries.* Edinburgh: T. & A. Constable, 1927.
'Bosvile of Ravenfield', *R & D.F.H.S.N.* **1**, 1984, unpaginated (3pp). Medieval-19th c.

Boswell

BOSWELL, JAMES JASPER. *History and genealogical tables of the Boswells: their ancient alliances and connections from the founder of the name in the year 1066 to this date, 1906.* [ ], 1906. Includes pedigrees. Extensive.

Bottomley

BURAY, MONIQUE. 'A difficult line: the Bottomleys', *Y.F.H.* **18**(4), 1992, 91-3. 19th c.

Boumphrey
See Rodes

Bourchier

MURRAY, HUGH. 'Rainwater hoods and fallpipe brackets, part III', *Y.A.S., F.H.P.S.S.N.* **5**(2), 1979, 29. Bourchier family; includes pedigrees, 16-18th c.
TAYLOR, PAT. 'The Restoration Bourchiers of Beninbrough Grange', *Y.A.J.* **60**, 1988, 127-47. Includes pedigree, 17-18th c., also probate inventory of Sir Barrington Bourchier, 1695.

Bower

BOWER, IRENE MARY. 'Who are you, John?', *Bod-Kin* **39**, 1995, 21-4. Bower family, 18-19th c.

Bowlby

HILL, WILLIAM J. 'Seven generations of the Bowlby family from Helmsley, England', *Ryedale historian* **3**, 1967, 33-41. 16-18th c.

Bowne
See Field

Bowser
WAGNER, ANTHONY RICHARD, SIR. *The family of Bowser: genealogical researches with particular reference to Bowser of Yorkshire from medieval times.* Glasgow: Robert MacLehose and Co., 1966. 15-20th c., includes extensive 'lists and abstracts of records searched'.

Boyle
BOYLE, M.B. 'Fair befall the flax field: aspects of the history of the Boyle family and their flax business', in *Thoresby miscellany* 17. *T.S.* **56**. 1981, 1-26. 18-20th c.
'Family photograph album', *Don. Anc.* **6**(6), 1994, 156. Lists portraits in an album of the Boyle and Scriven families of Leeds.

Boynton
COLLIER, CARUS VALE. *An account of the Boynton family, and the family seat of Burton Agnes.* Middlesborough: William Appleyard & Sons, 1914. Also of Barmston, Hunmanby and Sedbury; includes pedigrees, medieval-19th c., and monumental inscriptions at Burton Agnes.

Braddyll
See Talbot

Bradford
BROWNE, WILLIAM BRADFORD. 'Ancestry of the Bradfords of Austerfield, Co. York', *New England historical and genealogical register* **83**, 1929, 439-64; **84**, 1930, 5-17. 16th c., includes wills, parish register extracts, *etc.*
BROWNE, WILLIAM BRADFORD. 'The English ancestry of William Bradford, governor of Plymouth Colony', *Genealogists magazine* **6**, 1932-4, 142-5. Originally of Yorkshire, 16th c.
CUDWORTH, WILLIAM. 'The Bradford family', *B.A.* **2**, 1895, 127-30. 15-16th c.

Bradfourth
SOMERBY, H.G. 'Extracts from the register books of Austerfield, in Yorkshire 1561-1631', *New England historical & genealogical register* **4**, 1850, 177-8. Concerning the Bradfourth and Morton families.

Bradley
LAW, E.J. 'The Bradley family and their Newhouse', *O.W.R.* **5**(2), 1985, 22-7. In Huddersfield, 18-19th c.

Bradshaw
See Vescy

Bram(m)all
PERKINS, JOHN P. 'Bramall', *F.S.* **3**(1), 1981, 21-3. 16-19th c.
See also Leckey

Brass
BRASS, JAMES O.L. 'A one name study', *J.Cl.F.H.S.* **1**(3), 1981, 68-70. Brass family.

Brearcliffe
HANSON, T.W. 'John Brearcliffe the antiquary: the Brearcliffe family', *P.R.H.A.S.* 1907, 227-41. 17-18th c., includes folded pedigree.

Breckon
BRECKON, CHARLES. 'My first year of family history', *J.Cl.F.H.S.* **1**(5), 1981, 122-3. Breckon family, 18-19th c.

Brewster
HUNT, JOHN G. 'The mother of Elder William Brewster of the Mayflower', *New England historical and genealogical register* **124**, 1970, 150-6. Brewster family, 16th c., also includes note on Grene family of Barnby upon Don.

Brigg(s)
See Newson and Thoresby

Brise
See Way

Broadbent
BROADBENT, L. 'Carrhead, Carr and Lee farms in pre-Victorian times', *B.S.H.S.* **21**(3), 1991, 2-7. Broadbent family of Saddleworth; includes pedigree 17-19th c.
See also Hall

Brocas
'Sir Bernard Brocas the younger, son of Sir Bernard Brocas and Agnes Vavasour', *M.G.H.* 5th series **10**, 1938, 98-9. 14th c.

Brodrick
BRODRICK, J.J. 'The family of Cuthbert Brodrick', *B.T.* **41**, 1990, 13-14. See also **42**, 1990, 7. 19-20th c.
MIDLETON, VISCOUNT. 'Brodrick genealogy', *M.G.H.* **2**, 1876, 359-70. Of Yorkshire, Surrey, *etc.*, medieval-19th c.

Brook(e)
FISK, MICHAEL B. 'Grandfather Brook (1881-1975)', *H. & D.F.H.S.J.* **6**(3), 1993, 86-8. Brook family, 17-20th c.
LAWSON-TANCRED, THOMAS, SIR. 'The township of Ellenthorpe and the Brooke family', *Y.A.J.* **34**, 1939, 73-9. Includes pedigree, 17-18th c.
PHILLIPS, S.E.L. 'Brook of Newhouse, Huddersfield, Yorkshire', *Y.A.S., F.H.P.S.S.N.* **3**(3), 1977, 44-6. 16-17th c.
TOMLINSON, G.W. 'Brooke family', *M.G.H.* 2nd series **5**, 1894, 255-63. Of Huddersfield; includes pedigree, 16-18th c., with 18th c. wills.
TOMLINSON, G.W. 'Pedigree of the family of Brooke of Newhouse in the parish of Huddersfield, and Dodsworth in the parish of Silkstone, in the West Riding of Yorkshire', *Y.A.J.* **12**, 1893, 405-12. Includes wills of John Brooke, 1753, and John Chas. Brooke, 1790.

Brooksbank
REDMONDS, GEORGE. 'Surname history: Brooksbank', *H. & D.F.H.S.J.* **6**(2), 1993, 71.
SEALS, W.F. 'The Brooksbanks of Elland', *T.Hal.A.S.* 1970, 71-9. 14-18th c.

Bright
LIPSON, ERIC. 'The Brights of Market Place', *T.Hunter A.S.* **6**, 1950, 117-25. Sheffield, 18-19th c.
PORTER, WILLIAM S. *Notes on the Hallamshire family of Bright.* [Sheffield]: [Sheffield Miscellany], 1897. Reprinted from the *Sheffield Miscellany.* 15-19th c., includes pedigrees.

Broadbent
BARROW, NEIL. 'The origins of the Broadbents of Saddleworth', *B.S.H.S.* **20**(2), 1990, 19-21. 15-16th c.

BROADBENT, LEONARD. 'The Broadbents in Diglee, 16th to mid-19th century', *B.S.H.S.* **23**(4), 1993, 7-19. Includes pedigree.

Brocas
BURROWS, MONTAGU. *The family of Brocas of Beaurepaire and Roche Court, hereditary masters of royal buckhounds ...* Longmans Green and Co., 1886. Medieval-19th c., includes folded pedigree, with abstracts of 462 deeds relating to Hampshire, Berkshire, Surrey and Yorkshire, *etc.*

Brontë
LEYLAND, FRANCIS A. *The Brontë family with special reference to Patrick Branwell Brontë.* Hunt and Blackett, 1886. Reprinted Didsbury: E.J. Marten, 1973. 19th c.
The Brontës then and now. A symposium of articles reprinted from various issues of the Brontë Society transactions, and now published as a Jane Eyre and Wuthering Heights centenary tribute. Shipley: Outhwaite Bros., [for the Brontë Society], 1947.

Brooksbank
SHEPHERD, E.M. *Brooksbank: yeomen of the Dales (their times, friends and connections).* [ ]: the author, [1989]. Includes pedigree, 16-18th c.

Broomhead
See Marsden

Brougham
WYLY, PETER & STACEY, PEGGY. 'The Broughams of Askrigg - and elsewhere!' *Cumbria Family History Society Newsletter* **59**, 1991 10-14. Includes pedigree 17-10th c.

Broughton
JACKSON, CHARLES. 'Autobiographical memoir of the Rev. Thomas Broughton', *Y.A.J.* **4**, 1877, 377-83. Includes 'genealogical notices of the Broughton family', 17-19th c.
See also Bullen

Browne
BROWN, JEAN K. 'With more than a little bit of luck', *Bod-Kin* **40**, 1995, 18-19. Browne family, 18-20th c.

Brownridge
MOORE, EDNA M. 'The Brownridge family of Leeds', *Y.F.H.* **15**(3), 1989, 83-4. 19-20th c.

Buck
'Pedigree of Buck, from Dugdale's *Visitation of Yorkshire,* with additions from other sources', *Y.C.M.* **1**, 1891, 337-8. 17-18th c.
See also Humble

Buckley
FISHWICK, HENRY. *A genealogical memorial of the family of Buckley of Derby and Saddleworth, in the counties of Derby and York, with appendices: abstract of wills, Chancery proceedings, inquis. post mort., &c.* Privately printed, 1900. Includes pedigrees, 16-19th c.
JAGGER, H. 'The Buckly family of Saddleworth', *B.S.H.S.* **2**(2), 1972, 25-6.

Buckroyd
See Ackroyd

Bullen
FRANKLYN, CHARLES A.H. *The genealogy of Anne the Queen (Anne Bullen) and other English families, including Broughton of Impens, North Petherton, Co. Somerset, Pontifex of West Wycombe, Co. Buckingham, Waddington of Mexborough, Co. York, Walwyn of Kilmersdon and Frome, Co. Somerset, and of Bognor Regis, Co. Sussex* ... [Privately printed], 1977.

Bunny
BANKS, W.S. 'On entries relating to the Bunny family, in the Normanton parish register', *Y.A.J.* **3**, 1875, 8-25. 16-17th c.

Burgh
POLLARD, A.J. 'The Burghs of Brough Hall, c.1270-1540', *Journal* **6**, N.Y.C.R.O.P. **17**, 1978, 5-34. Includes pedigree.
WALKER, J.W. 'The Burghs of Cambridgeshire and Yorkshire, and the Watertons of Lincolnshire and Yorkshire', *Y.A.J.* **30**, 1931, 311-419. Includes folded pedigrees, medieval-19th c.

Burling
See Field

Burnett
LOWREY, LINDA. 'The Burnett family of Yeadon, Guiseley, Yorkshire', *Y.F.H.* **15**(5), 1989, 127-31. 19-20th c., includes pedigree.

Burnley
PRESTON, W.E. 'Burnley of Eccleshill', *B.A.* N.S. **3**, 1912, 410. Pedigree, 16-17th c.

Burrell
See Stickney

Burrows
See Barras

Burton
CAHILL, BRENDA. 'Taken from a family bible', *F.S.* **6**(4), 1986, 95. Burton and Pollard families of Hickleton and Sprotborough, mid-19th c.
RODGER, MARGERY. 'Burton', *F.S.* **2**(2), 1979, 47-50. Medieval family.
'The Burton family of Clifton, York: refs. giving connection between Newton and Clifton branches', *Y.A.S., F.H.P.S.S.N.* **12**, 1974, 4-10. 16-18th c. (Newton on Ouse)

Busfeild
See Atkinson

Bygod
MOOR, CHARLES. 'The Bygods, Earls of Norfolk', *Y.A.J.* **32**, 1936. 172-213. Medieval, includes pedigrees.

Bygott
BYGOTT, R.C. 'One thousand years of a family history', *B.T.* **77**, 1999, 33-6; **78**, 1999, 32-4. Bygott family history.
See also Colver

Byrom
BRADBURY, ALLAN. 'The Byrom family of Slackcote', *B.S.H.S.* **25**(2), 1995, 17-18. Late 19th c.

Caedmon
See Sedman

Calverley
WALLING, GLORIA. 'Always note the witnesses names', *Y.F.H.* **23**(3) 1997, 71-2. Calverley family, 19th c.
WALLING, GLORIA. 'The New Zealand connection', *Y.F.H.* **23**(5), 1997, 109-13. Calverley family, 19th c.
See also Blackett and Royd(s)

Calvert
COAKLEY, THOMAS M. 'George Calvert, first Lord Baltimore: family, status, arms', *Maryland historical magazine* **79**(3), 1984, 255-69. Not seen. Genealogical study.
See also Crossland

Campnett
ROBERTS, FRANK. 'The Campnetts of Huddersfield', *Y.F.H.* **15**(5), 1989, 117-20. Includes pedigree, 19-20th c.

Capstick
See Hartley

Carethorpe
See Scrope

Carew
LUMB, G. DENISON. 'Carew-Shepley', *M.G.H.* 2nd series **4**, 1892, 321-3. Of Lisbon, Portugal, and Yorkshire, 18th c.

Carl(e)ton
HAZEN, TRACY ELLIOT. 'The English ancestry of Edward Carlton, of Rowley, Mass', *New England historical and genealogical register* **93**, 1939, 1-46. See also **96**, 1942, 197-8 & **106**, 1952, 89. Includes folded pedigree of Carleton of Beeford and Brandesburton, *etc.*, 16-17th c. with numerous extracts from wills, parish registers, lay subsidies, deeds, *etc.*
See also Newton

Caroline
SPENCER, WILLIAM E. 'Sailors and sundries', *Y.F.H.* **18**(4), 1992, 98-101. Caroline family, 18-19th c.

Carr(e)
ADDY, S.O. 'The Carrs of Southey and Dublin', *T.Hunter A.S.* **3**, 1929, 273-94. Includes pedigrees of Carr, 16-19th c., and Marsh of Darton, 16th c., with will abstracts.

C. 'Carre of Sleaford and Carr of Stackhouse', *Genealogist* **3**, 1879, 380-6. 15-17th c. Sleaford is in Lincolnshire.
CHANDLER, MARY. 'My Yorkshire roots', *K.D.F.H.S.J.* Autumn 1996, 19-21. Carr family, 18-20th c.

Carter
REDMONDS, GEORGE. 'Surname history: Carter', *H. & D.F.H.S.J.* **6**(1), 1992, 35.
RUSBY, J. 'Carter of Thorpe Audlin', *Y.G.* **1**, 1888, 195-8. Notes on wills and extracts from Badsworth parish register, *etc.*, 16-17th c.
WRIGHT, W.BALL. 'Carter of Yorkshire, Manchester, and Ireland', *Pedigree register* **2**, 1910-13, 204-11. Includes pedigree, 17-19th c., with will and deed abstracts.

Carver
CLAGUE, CHERYL. 'My Carver connections', *Y.F.H.* **15**(6), 1989, 157-60. 18-19th c.
DONALD, JOYCE B. 'The Carver family', *T.Hal.A.S.* 1971, 123-32. 17-19th c.

Casson
See Richardson

Cattley
COVENEY, GERALD M. 'The Cattleys of Bramham', *O.W.R.* **5**(2), 1985, 24-7. 18th c.
COVENEY, GERALD. 'The Cattleys in Russia', *O.W.R.* **6**(2), 1986, 22-4.

Cave
COOPER, T.P. *The Caves of York: topographical draughtsmen, artists, engraver, and copper-plate printers.* York: Art Gallery, 1934. Includes pedigree, 18-19th c.

Cayvill
ELLIS, A.S. 'Notes on some ancient East Riding families and their arms', *T.E.R.A.S.* **4**, 1896, 66-71. On the Cayvills of Cayvill and the De Murers of Elvington, medieval.

Cellarer
KENNEDY, MARJORIE J.O. 'Resourceful villeins: the Cellarer family of Wawne in Holderness', *Y.A.J.* **48**, 1976, 107-17. 13-14th c.

Chandler
SMITH, MARGARET D. 'Chandler family bible', *R.H.* 4(1), 1999, 15-16. 19-20th c.

Charlesworth
HUGHES, JOHN. 'The cousins came to town', *F.S.* 19(4), 1998, 145-6. Charlesworth family, 18-19th c.
'The Charlesworths of Bankbottom, being the reminiscences of Joe Charlesworth of Marsden, set down by his wife Alice Maude in 1945', *O.W.R.* 4(1), 1984, 8-10.
See also Fenton

Chauncy
TUCKER, STEPHEN. 'Pedigree of the family of Chauncy', *M.G.H.* 2nd series 1, 1886, 21-30. Of Yorkshire, Hertfordshire, *etc.*, 13-18th c.

Chaytor
ELWES, DUDLEY CARY. 'Chaytor', *M.G.H.* N.S., 3, 1880, 64. Of Richmond (probably the Yorkshire one); entries from a 17th c. bible.

Chedzoy
See Leckey

Cherry
STRENSALL, JOHN CHERRY. '14th & 15th century Hull and the Cherry family', *Y.F.H.* 20(6), 1994, 138-40.

Chew
CRESSWELL, VERA. 'The Chew family of Morley', *Cameo* 1994, no. 1, 5-6; 1994, no. 2, 7. 18-19th c.

Cheyney
See De La Vache

Cholmley
GASKIN, R.T. 'The Cholmleys of Whitby', *B.A.* N.S. 1, 1905, 418-62. 16-17th c.
GASKIN, R.T. 'The Cholmleys of Whitby', *B.A.* N.S., 2, 1905, 418-62. 16-17th c.
PEARSON, F.R. *The Abbey House, Whitby, under the Cholmley family.* Whitby: Horne & Son, 1954. Originally published as *The Abbey House, Whitby,* 1929. 16-19th c.

'Cholmley: extracts from the Cholmley bible, Whitby Abbey', *M.G.H.* 2, 1876, 220-22. 17-18th c., includes Whitby parish register extracts.
See also Legard

Clapham
CLAPHAM, BARBARA. *The Clapham family: the ancient family of Clapham; the Claphams of Beamsley, Co. York; the Claphams of Batley & Birstall.* The author, 1993. Medieval-20th c.
CLAPHAM, JOHN ARTHUR. 'Some Claphams of note', *B.A.* N.S., 3, 1912, 213-23. 17-19th c.
C., J.A. 'The Clapham family', *Y.G.* 2, 1890, 71-4. Medieval.
'Clapham', *Y.G.* 1, 1888, 224-8. Includes folded pedigree of Clapham of Clapham, Beamsley, Cottingley, Leeds and Bradford, medieval-19th c.
'The Clapham family', *Old Yorkshire* 1, 1881, 218-20. Medieval-19th c.
'Clapham of Feizor', *Y.G.* 1, 1888, 189-90. Pedigree, 17-19th c.
'Pedigree of Clapham of Clapham, Beamsley, Leeds and Bradford', *Y.N.Q.II.* 1, 1905, 376-7. 18-20th c.
See also Hall

Clark
BRAMLEY, D.M. 'The Clark family of Doncaster', *Don. Anc.* 2(1), 1983, 18-19. 19th c.

Clarkson
Y., N. 'Clarksons of Bradford', *Y.G.* 1, 1888, 163-6. Includes pedigree, 17th c.

Clayton
See hall

Clegg
See Royds

Clifford
CLAY, J.W. 'The Clifford family', *Y.A.J.* 18, 1904-5, 354-411. Includes pedigree, medieval-17th c.
CLIFFORD, ARTHUR. *Collectanea Cliffordiana.* Arthur Clifford, 1817. Reprinted Skipton: Skipton Castle, 1980. Somewhat fanciful, but of great interest.

CLIFFORD, HUGH. *The house of Clifford of Clifford Castle, Skipton, Chudleigh from before the Conquest.* Chichester: Phillimore, 1987.

HOYLE, R.W. 'The first Earl of Cumberland a reputation re-assessed', *N.H.* **22**, 1986, 63-94. Clifford family.

HUNTLEY, LOCKWOOD. *The Cliffords of Skipton Castle.* Historic Yorkshire families series. New ed. York: North of England Newspaper Co., 1906. Reprinted from the *Yorkshire gazette.*

JAMES, M.E. 'The first Earl of Cumberland (1493-1342) and the decline of northern feudalism, *N.H.* **1**, 1966, 43-69. General study of Clifford family influence.

SPENCE, R.T. 'A noble funeral in the Great Civil War', *Y.A.J.* **65**, 1993, 115-23. Account of the funeral of Henry Clifford, Earl of Cumberland, 1643.

Close
B[RUCE], W.D. 'The Close family of Richmond, Yorkshire', *Topographer & genealogist* **1**, 1846, 557-61.

Clough
See Smith

Coates
GREEN, EVERARD. 'Pedigree of the family of Coates, of Helperby Hall, and of Thornton-le-Beans, and Pasture House, both in the parish of North Otterington in the North Riding of the County of York', *M.G.H.* 4th series **2**, 1908, 181-9. 16-19th c.

SMITH, AVIS. *My Nidderdale and area ancestors, Yorkshire, England.* Rosebud West, Victoria: Avis Smith, 1995. Coates, Gill, Habishaw, Haw, Hickham, King, Storey, Umpleby and Wilkinson families, 18-19th c.

'Coates of Kildwick', *Y.C.M.* **2**, 1892, 239-40. Includes pedigree, 16-18th c.

See also Smith

Cockcroft
COCKCROFT, W. LAWSON. 'Where there's a will', *Y.F.H.* **21**(4), 1995, 90-92. Cockcroft family, 18-19th c.

COCKCROFT, W. LAWSON. 'Finding father's family', *Y.F.H.* **18**(1), 1992, 183-8. 18-20th c.

Cocker
DALBY, MARK. *The Cocker connection: Yorkshire, Van Diemans Land, Melbourne, British Columbia, Mexico, Tonga and Michigan.* Regency Press, 1989. 18-20th c

DALBY, MARK. 'The Cockers of Almondbury', *H. & D.F.H.S.J.* **2**(2), 1989. 41. 19th c.

Cockhill
See Cocking

Cocking
REDMONDS, GEORGE. 'Surname history: Cocking and Cockhill', *H. & D.F.H.S.J.* **4**(1), 1990, 39.

Cockshott
GILLER, C.A. 'Pedigree of Cockshott', *K.D.F.H.S.J.* Spring 1997, 14-15. 18-20th c.

Cockson
COCKSON, ALAN. 'Notes on early Cockson families in middle Wharfedale', *Wh.N.* **13**, 1994, 14-17.

COCKSON, ALAN. 'Occcasional notes on Yorkshire Cockson families', *Wh.N.* **12**, 1994, 16-19. 18-19th c.

Coghill
COGHILL, JAMES HENRY. *The family of Coghill, 1377 to 1879, with some sketches of their maternal ancestors, the Slingbys of Scriven Hall, 1135 to 1879.* Cambridge: Riverside Press, 1879. Originally from Knaresborough; junior branches were of London, Bletchingdon (Oxfordshire), the United States, Hertfordshire, *etc.*

Coldbeck
WELLSTED, W.A. 'The Coldbecks of Batley', *Y.F.H.* **18**(1), 1992, 171-4. 18-19th c.

Coldwell
REDMONDS, GEORGE. 'Surname history: Coldwell', *H. & D.F.H.S.J.* **2**(1), 1988, 27.

Cole
LOCKE, CHARLES. 'Two brothers named Cole', *Bod-Kin* **20**, 1990, 8-9. 19th c.

WOODALL, IRIS. 'Family bible', *J.Cl.F.H.S.* **4**(1), 1989, 34-6. Reprinted from *B.T.* Entries relating to the Cole, Trattles, Jenkinson, Crawford, Moor and Edmond families, 19th c.

'Family bible', *B.T.* **28**, 1986, 9. Entries relating to the families of Cole, Trattles, Moore, Jenkinson and Crawford, 19th c., from bible found in a Weaversthorpe cottage.

Collingwood
'Bay Hall, Huddersfield, in connexion with Collingwood, Walker and Rushforth', *Y.A.J.* **12**, 1893, 267(f). Folded pedigree, 18-19th c.

Collins
COLLINS, FRANCIS. *The family of Collins of Knaresborough, with some of their connexions.* Leeds: J. Whitehead and Son, 1912. 17-20th c.; also includes pedigrees of many related families.
See also Furniss

Coltman
CLARKSON, DESMOND. 'Long lost relatives', *C.Y.D.F.H.S.N.* **18**, 1988, 12-13. Includes pedigree of Coltman and Armitage, 19-20th c.

Colton-Fox
See Rodes

Colver
NUTTING, DAVID C. *The Colvers of Hallamshire, to the 17th century and beyond, including the lines of Nicholson, Bygott, Porter, Nutting, Swift.* 2nd ed. Chichester: David Colver, 1995.

Colville
'Pedigree of the Colvilles of Arncliffe, Sigston, Dale, East Heslerton and Lutton in the County of York, of St Helens Auckland in the County of Durham, and of Butill and Spindelston in Northumberland', *Y.A.J.* **10**, 1889, 167-8.

Conn
CONN, D.A. 'The Conn family of Upleatham', *J.Cl.F.H.S.* **3**(7), 1987, 33-6.

Connolly
DAYNES, SUSAN. 'Pedigree of Connolly', *K.D.F.H.S.J.* Spring 1998, 14-15. 18-20th c.

Consitt
CONSITT, F. JOHN P. 'Francis Consitt: an engraver of York, with overtures in Canada', *C.Y.D.F.H.S.N.* **18**, 1988, 16-22. 16-10th c.

Constable
BOULTER, W. CONSITT. 'Constable of S. Sepulchre's, Yorkshire', *M.G.H.* N.S., **1**, 1874, 63 & 99. Extracts from Preston and Hedon parish registers, 16-17th c.
CLAY, CHARLES. 'Notes on the early generations of the family of Constable of Halsham', *Y.A.J.* **40**, 1962, 197-204. 11-12th c., also includes notes on the Alost family.
ELLIS, A.S. 'Notes on some ancient East Riding families and their arms, IX: the Constables of Flamborough', *T.E.R.A.S.* **12**, 1905, 1-9. Medieval.
HERRIES, LORD. 'The Constables of Flamborough', *T.E.R.A.S.* **8**, 1900, 51-69. Constable family, medieval-16th c.
ROEBUCK, PETER. 'The Constables of Everingham: the fortunes of a Catholic family during the Civil War and Interregnum', *Recusant history* **9**, 1967-8, 75-87.
Burton Constable Hall: the eighteenth and nineteenth centuries. E.Y.L.H.S. **56**. 1998. Includes pedigree of Constable, 17-19th c.
'Constable of Everingham', *Y.G.* **2**, 1890, 135-40. Pedigree, 13-18th c.
'Constable pedigree, of Flamborough', *Y.G.* **2**, 1890, 131-4. 12-17th c.
See also Legard

Cook(e)
COOKE, DAVID, SIR. 'The Cookes of Wheatley', *Don. Anc.* **3**(4), 1987, 125-33. 15-19th c., includes list of household staff from 1851 census.
COOKE, DAVID, SIR. 'Famous families and homes around Doncaster. Cooke of Wheatley', *Don. Anc.* **4**(6), 1991, 187-92; **5**(1), 1991, 221-20. 16-20th c.
FLECK, ROD. 'The Australasian Society for Descendents of the Cook / Fleck family', *J.Cl.F.H.S.* **3**(11), 1988, 37-40.
See also Davies-Cooke and Way

Copley

BAILDON, W. PALEY. 'Notes on the early pedigree of the Copley family', *Miscellanea* [8]. *T.S.* **26**, 1924, 350-71; *Miscellanea* [9]. *T.S.* **28**, 1928, 195-211. Medieval.

CORBETT, J.A. 'The Corbetts at Wortley', *F.S.* **12**(4), 1992, 102-3. Brief note, 16-18th c.

Corker

CORKER, T.M. 'Corker: an old Northumbrian family', *Y.A.J.* **28**, 1926, 89-92. Includes wills of James Corker of Huntwicke, 1573, and Elizabeth Corker, 1590.

Cottrell

See Way

Coward

TAYLOR, HOWARD 'The Coward family and the bleach-works at Swithen', *O.W.R.* **12**, 1992, 3-5. 18-19th c.

Craven

STAVERT, W.J. 'Notes on the pedigree of the Cravens of Appletreewick', *Y.A.J.* **13**, 1895, 440-80. Includes pedigrees and extracts from parish registers, subsidy rolls, probate records, *etc.*

'My Craven ancestors', *K.D.F.H.S.J.* Autumn 1992, 6. Pedigree shewing descent of Craven, Simms, Dawson, Ayrton, Jackson and Postlethwaite, 16-20th c.

Crawshaw

HAWKSWORTH, JOHN. 'Crawshaws of Wentworth: a tale from New Zealand', *F.S.* **13**(4), 1993, 97-8. 19-20th c.

Crawford

See Coles

Crawthorne

See Roberts

Creyke

'The family of Creyke', *Old Yorkshire* 2nd series **2**, 1890, 144-9. 14-19th c.

See also Legard

Crispin

CRISPIN, M. JACKSON. 'The Crispins of Kingston-on-Hull', *Publications of the Genealogical Society of Pennsylvania* **10**(2), 1928, 105-22. 16-17th c.

Croft

CARLISLE, NICHOLAS. *Notices of the ancient family of Croft of the counties of Lancaster and York.* Shakespeare Press, 1841. Medieval-19th c.

Crofton

CROFTON, HENRY THOMAS. et al. *Crofton memoirs: an account of John Crofton, Queen Elizabeth's escheator-general of Ireland, and of his ancestors and others bearing the name.* York: Yorkshire Printing Company, 1911. Of Cumberland, London, Yorkshire, Buckinghamshire, Lincolnshire, *etc.*

Crosby

PRINDLE, PAUL W. 'The Yorkshire ancestry of the three Crosby sisters of Rowley, Mass.', *New England historical and genealogical register* **119**, 1964, 243-8. See also **120**, 1966, 225-7. 15-17th c.

See also Watson

Crosland

'Quaker families: Crosland families', *Y.C.M.* **1**, 1891, 293. Pedigree, 18-19th c.

Crosskill

BROWN, G. PHILIP. 'Crosskills of Beverley', in CROWTHER, JAN, & CROWTHER, PETER, eds. *Collected Essays from the Bulletin of the East Yorkshire Local History Society, nos. 1-55, 1970 - Feb. 1997.* [ ]: The Society, 1977, vol. 1, 35-7. Originally published in the *Bulletin* **24**, 1982, 7-9. 18-19th c.

Crossland

CULVER, FRANCIS B. 'Maternal ancestry of Sir George Calvert', *Maryland historical magazine* **29**, 1934, 330-31. Not seen. Crossland family of Almondbury.

Crossley

BRETTON, R. 'Crossleys of Dean Clough', *T. Hal.A.S.* 1950, 1-9; 1951, 71-83; 1952, 49-58; 1953, 1-20 & 87-102; 1954, 11-28. 18-20th c.

CROSSLEY, E.W. 'Crossleys of Scaitcliffe', *P.R.H.A.S.* 1907, 218-26. 14-17th c.

WEBSTER, ERIC. 'The record of a continuous progress: the 19th century development of John Crossley and Sons, carpet manufacturers of Halifax', *Industrial archaeology* **16**(1), 1981, 58-72.

'The late Mr. James Crossley', *Palatine notebook* **3**, 1883, 221-8. Includes pedigree of Crossley of Lancashire and Yorkshire, etc., 17-19th c.

Cudworth
CUDWORTH, WILLIAM. 'Noted Bradford lawyers, I: the Cudworth family', *B.A.* **1**, 1888, 247-53. Includes pedigree, 18-19th c.

GREEN, JOSEPH JOSHUA. *Some account of the family of Cudworth of Yorkshire, Lancashire, etc., particularly of that branch settled at Sandal Magna, near Wakefield, Co. York, and Darlington, Co. Durham, circa 1630-1898.* Headley Brothers, 1898. Includes pedigrees.

Culling
'Mark my words ...! (The Cullings of Campsall)', *Don. Anc.* **9**(4), 1998, 100-102. 19-20th c.

Cusworth
'George Cusworth', *Don. Anc.* **6**(3), 1993, 72-3. Includes list of research materials on the Cusworth family, now in Doncaster Archives.

Cutsforth
MEILAHN, ELIZABETH CUTSFORTH. *Cutsforth ancestry in England and America: includes allied lines of Robson, Gavin and Gray: a genealogical study.* 3rd revision. Chetek, Wisconsin: the author, 1985.

Dale
DALE, HYLTON B. 'Dale: Hands', *Pedigree register* **1**, 1907-10, 12-13. Of Whitby, London, etc., pedigree, 18-19th c.

Dalton
DALTON, CHARLES. 'The family of Dalton', *M.G.H.* N.S., **3**, 1880, 438-9. 15-19th c.

Danby
WHONE, CLIFFORD. 'Christopher Danby of Masham and Farnley (who resided at Leighton Hall)', in *Thoresby Miscellany* **11**. *T.S.* **37**, 1945, 1-29. Includes folded pedigree, 15-18th c.

'Danby v. Sydenham: a Restoration Chancery suit', *Y.A.J.* **17**, 1901-2, 72-93. Includes inscription relating to Dakins and Hoby; also pedigrees showing relationships.

Daniel
DANIEL, ROBERT. 'Across the Civil War divide', *Family tree magazine* **8**(10), 1992, 27-8. Daniel family; includes notes on a variety of pre-Civil War sources in Yorkshire.

Darby
See Smith

Dartmouth
See Legge

Davies-Cooke
USHER, GWILYM ARTHUR. *Gwysaney and Oulston: a history of the family of Davies-Cooke of Gwysaney, Flintshire, and Owston, West Riding of Yorkshire.* Denbigh: the author, 1964. Medieval-20th c., includes pedigrees, and chapter on 'The Cookes of Owston.'

Davy
DAVY, HENRY DENNIS. *Davy of Steeton and Keighley.* Newcastle-upon-Tyne: privately printed, 1979. Includes folded pedigrees, 14-20th c.

Dawnay
See Legard

Dawson
DITCHFIELD, P.H. *The history of the Dawson family of Farlington and North Ferriby, York., of Ackworth Park and Osgodby Hall in the County of York; of Greystoke, Cumberland, of Arborfield House, Berkshire and of Philadelphia, United States of America.* G. Allen & Co., [191-?]

REDMONDS, GEORGE. 'Surname history: Dawson', *H.D.F.H.S.J.* **1**(1), 1987, 19.

'Dawson pedigree', *M.G.H.* **2**, 1876, 51-4. 16-17th c., includes monumental inscriptions.

See also Craven, Humble and Stickney

Dawtrey
BROADBENT, STEVE. 'Where did my Dawtreys go - and where did they come from?' *Y.F.H.* **23**(5), 1997, 124-6. 19th c.

De Araine
See Aske

De La Pole

CHINNERY, MARIE. 'The De La Poles of Kingston-upon-Hull: their origins and early years', *Blanc Sanglier* 9(2), 1975, 6-14; 9(3), 1975, 10-14; 10(1), 1975, 2-7; 10(2), 1976, 12-16.

HARVEY, A.S. *The De La Pole family of Kingston upon Hull*. York: East Yorkshire Local History Society, 1957. 14-16th c.

HARVEY, A.S. *The homeland of the De La Poles: Kingston upon Hull and Wingfield in Suffolk*. Hull: privately published, 1934. Medieval, includes folded pedigree.

HORROX, ROSEMARY. *The De La Poles of Hull*. E.Y.L.H.S. 38. 1983. Includes pedigrees, 14-15th c.

HUNTLEY, LOCKWOOD. *Ravenser and the rise of the De La Pole family of Hull*. 2nd ed. Beverley: Green & Son, 1914. Medieval.

RAVEN, JOHN JAMES. 'History of the De La Poles', *Suffolk Institute of Archaeology* 7, 1891, 51-6. Medieval.

TRAVIS-COOK, J. *The story of the De La Poles*. Hull: Eastern Morning News, 1888. Medieval, includes pedigree.

De La Pryme

EGAR, S. 'De La Pryme', *Fenland notes and queries* 4, 1898-1900, 73-6. 17-18th c. Huguenot family.

De La Vache

H., W. 'De La Vache, Restwold and Cheyney', *M.G.H.* 2, 1876, 134-5. Of Buckinghamshire, Yorkshire, *etc.*, pedigree, 14-18th c.

De Murer

See Cayvill

De Ros

HAWKESBURY, LORD. 'The heraldry on the gateway at Kirkham Abbey', *T.E.R.A.S.* 8, 1900, 1-9. Medieval; includes 'skeleton pedigree of the De Ros family ... to show descent to the present day of that family and of the present owner of Kirkham,' 'Sir William De Ros of Ingmanthorpe', *M.G.H.* 5th series 10, 1938, 20. 13th c.

Dearman

See Atkinson and Smith

Denison

BODDINGTON, REGINALD STEWART. 'Pedigree of the family of Denison', *M.G.H.* 2nd series 1, 1886, 148. See also 180 & 248. Of Yorkshire and Surrey, 18-19th c.

HEWLINGS, RICHARD. 'Denison Hall, Little Woodhouse, Leeds', *Y.A.J.* 61, 1989, 173-80. See also 63, 1991, 220-21. Denison family, 17-18th c., includes many names of architects and craftsmen *etc.*, who worked on the house.

LUMB, G.D. 'The Denison family', in *Miscellanea* [8], *T.S.* 26, 1924, 103-5. 18th c.; includes will of William Denison, 1778.

LUMB, G.D. 'The family of Denison of Great Woodhouse, and their residences in Leeds', in *Miscellanea* [5], *T.S.* 15, 1909, 251-73. 16-18th c., includes pedigrees, wills, *etc.*

Dent

WARD, J.T. 'A nineteenth century Yorkshire estate: Ribston and the Dent family', *Y.A.J.* 41, 1966, 43-51.

Denton

MCPIKE, EUGENE FARFIELD. 'The Denton family', *Y.N.Q.II.* 5, 1908, 105-6. 19-20th c.

PRIESTLEY, J.H. 'The Denton family', *T.Hal.A.S.* 1957, 1-9. 14-20th c.

Dewhirst

ASHTON, JOHN R. 'All the trumpets sounded for him', *Bod-Kin* 20, 1990, 5-6. Dewhirst family, 19th c.

Dibnah

WATSON, KEVIN. 'The Dibnahs of Welwick', *B.T.* 29, 1987, 11-12. 16-19th c.

Dickon

KENZIE, KENNETH. 'The compliments slip', *Bod-Kin* 2(3), 1997, 21-4. See also 2(4), 1997, 19-20. Dickon family, 19th c.

WHITE, D.M. 'More than a tree', *B.T.* 72, 1997, 29-34. Dickon family of Hull, 18-19th c.

Dinsdale

DINSDALE, RICHARD. 'Clues but no evidence', *C.Y.D.F.H.S.J.* 43, 1997, 12-14. Dinsdale family of York, 17-18th c.

Dixon
'Dixon of Heaton Royds, Shipley', *Y.G.* **2**, 1890, 191. Pedigree, 17-18th c.
See also Smith

Dodson
BROOK, HILARY. 'Joseph Dodson of Birstall: tobacco pipe maker', *O.W.R.* **9**, 1989, 3-6. Includes pedigree, 18-19th c.

Doncaster
'Daniel Doncaster & Sons Limited: a brief history', *F.S.* 3(1), 1981, 11-12. 18-20th c.

Dodsworth
See Gray

Dormer
See Way

Dove
CONWAY, DUNCAN A. 'The Doves of Denby-in-Cleveland', *J.Cl.F.H.S.* 7(2), 1998, 36-8. 18-19th c.

Dowgill
'Rough sketches of Dowgill pedigree', *Y.C.M.* **4**, 1894, 185. Of Dowgill Hall, Ripley, 17-19th c.

D'Oyry
MAJOR, K. *The D'oyrys of South Lincolnshire, Norfolk and Holderness, 1130-1275.* Lincoln: the author, 1984. Includes pedigree.

Drake
COE, SHIELA. 'The Drake family, or what's in a name?', *Y.A.S., F.H.P.S.S.N.* 3(6), 1977, 93-5; 4(1), 1978, 106-8. Includes pedigree, 16-19th c.
LISTER, J. 'Horley Green', *P.R.H.A.S.* 1907, 93-112. At Halifax; Drake family, 13-19th c.
ROSS, FREDK. 'The Drake family', *Old Yorkshire* **5**, 1884, 186-91. 16-18th c.
See also Turner

Dransfield
REDMONDS, GEORGE. 'Surname history: Dransfield', *H. & D.F.H.S.J.* 3(3), 1990, 82.

Drury
DRURY, C. 'Pedigree of Drury', *M.G.H.* 5th series **2**, 1916-17, 117-8. 18-19th c.

Dufton
DUFTON, BERNARD. 'Dufton family research', *Y.F.H.* 16(1), 1990, 10-12. Medieval-19th c.

Duke
'The Dukes of Kimberworth', *R.& D.F.H.S.N.* **8**, 1986, unpaginated (4pp.) 18-19th c.

Dunhill
SATCHELL, TONY. *Linked by chains and lineage.* Ashburton, Vic.: T.Satchell, 1992. Dunhill family of Spaldington, 18-19th c.

Durance / Durrans
ATKIN, VALERIE. 'Thomas Durance / Durrans (1795-1849) and his family', *H. & D.F.H.S.J.* 8(3), 1995, 92-3.

Dyson
CROSSLEY, E.W. 'The Dyson family', *P.R.H.A.S.* 1917, 289-99, 1918, 165-92. 16-18th c., includes folded pedigree.
DYSON, MARK. 'The construction of a family', *H. & D.F.H.S.J.* 4(3), 1991, 80-81. Dyson family, 19th c.
YEATMAN, PYM. 'The Dysons of Swift Place in Sowerby', *Y.G.* **2**, 1890, 260-62. Includes pedigree, 16-19th c.

Earnshaw
REDMONDS, GEORGE. 'Surname history: Earnshaw', *H. & D.F.H.S.J.* 8(1), 1994, 35. Discussion of the surname.

Eastwood
KERSHAW W. DONALD. 'The joining together of two old Saddleworth families in 1881', *B.S.H.S.* 21(4), 1991, 18-19. Eastwood and Heginbottom families.
NEWELL, A. 'Eastwood and the Eastwood family', *P.R.H.A.S.* 1916, 145-67. Includes folded pedigree, 19-20th c.

Ecroyd
See Smith

Edmond
See Cole

Edwards
BENTLEY, G.E. 'The Edwardses of Halifax as booksellers by catalogue, 1749-1835', *Studies in bibliography* **45**, 1992, 187-222. Includes pedigree, 18-19th c.

EDWARDS, BERNARD. 'The Edwards of Northowram Hall', *Y.F.H.* 17(4), 1991, 96-100, 18-19th c.

EDWARDS, BERNARD. 'Edwards of Stainland II', *Y.F.H.* 15(6), 1989, 152-5. 19-20th c.

HANSON, T.W. 'Edwards of Halifax: a family of book-sellers, collectors and book-binders', *P.R.H.A.S.* 1912, 141-200. 18-19th c.

See also Atkinson

Elam

NEILL, NORMA. 'The Elams of Hillhouse', *O.W.R.* 5(1), 1985, 13-15 & 19-20. Includes pedigree, 18-19th c.

NEILL, NORMA. 'Unbelievable!' *Y.F.H.* 17(1), 1991, 10-12. Elam family, of Halifax and Leeds, 17-18th c.

Eland

CLAY, C.T. 'The family of Eland', *Y.A.J.* 27, 1924, 225-48. Includes pedigree, 12-13th c.

WILDRIDGE, THOMAS TINDALL. *The Eland family and their chantry in Holy Trinity: being five articles originally penned in the 'Chantries of Hull' in the 'Hull Times'.* Malet Lambert local history reprints. Extra vol. 17. Hull: Malet Lambert High School, 1981.

Elkington

ELKINGTON, ARTHUR E.H. & ELKINGTON, CHRISTINE M. *Early records of the name of Elkington in Lincolnshire and Yorkshire.* Banbury: The authors, 1965. Medieval.

Ellis

LUMB, G.D. 'Ellis of Kiddall', in *Miscellanea* [8]. *T.S.* 26, 1924, 61-3. 16-18th c.

POWELL, EDGAR. *Notes of one branch of the Ellis family in Yorkshire and Leicester-shire, with appendix and pedigree.* Privately published, 1905. Of Dinnington, 16-19th c.

REDMONDS, GEORGE. 'Surname history: Ellis', *H. & D.F.H.S.J.* 5(1), 1991, 35.

WADDINGTON, G.W. 'The Ellis family, and description of their manor hall at Kiddall, parish of Barwick-in-Elmet, County of York', in *Miscellanea* 1. *T.S.* 2. 1891, 55-61. Includes folded pedigree, 13-19th c.

WOOD, J.M. 'An Ellis family of Sheffield', *F.S.* 15(1), 1994, 14-15. 16-17th c.

Elmhirst

ELMHIRST, EDWARD. *Peculiar inheritance: a history of the Elmhirsts.* [ ], 1951. Includes pedigrees, 14-19th c.

See also Gray

Emerson

EMERSON, P.H. *The English Emersons: a genealogical historical sketch of the family from the earliest times to the end of the seventeenth century, including various modern pedigrees, with an appendix of authorities.* David Nutt, 1898. Of various counties, but especially of Co. Durham, London, Yorkshire, Northumberland, *etc., etc.,* medieval-19th c.

Emmott

Daus, ann. 'Who was Bernard?' *Wh.N.* 28, 1998, 17-20. Emmott family, 18-19th c.

Eskelby

ESHELBY, HENRY DOUGLAS. *The genealogy of the family of De Eskelby or Exelby, of the North Riding of the County of York.* [Birkenhead]: privately printed, 1891. Reprinted with additions from *Y.A.J.* 10 1889, 226-75, 423-30 & 482-501. Includes pedigrees, medieval-17th c., and numerous extracts from original sources, especially the Knaresborough manorial court rolls, 14-17th c.

ESHELBY, HENRY D. 'Notes on the genealogy of the family of de Eskelby, or Exelby, of Exelby and Disforth in the County of York', *Y.A.J.* 10, 1889, 266-75, 423-30 & 482-501. Includes medival pedigrees.

Eston

BEANLANDS, ARTHUR. 'The claim of John de Eston', in *Miscellanea* [7]. *T.S.* 24, 1919, 227-44. Medieval; includes folded pedigrees of Aveline de Forz, 11-13th c.

Eu

WATERS, EDMUND CHESTER. 'The Counts of Eu, sometime Lords of the Honour of Tickhill', *Y.A.J.* 9, 1986, 257-302 & 401-20. Includes pedigrees (one folded), 11-17th c.

Eure

BARKER, T. ELIZABETH. 'The Eure family', *Journal* 7; *N.Y.C.R.O.P.* 24, 1980, 21-66. Includes pedigree, 11-18th c.

JEWERS, ARTHUR J. 'Eure of Belton, Co. Lincoln', *Y.G.* 1, 1888, 67-70. Medieval, also of Yorkshire. Not completed.

Exelby

MOYLE, W.J.T. 'The Exelby family of St. Keverne', *Cornwall Family History Society journal* 5, 1977, 5-6; **16**, 1980, 3-4. Medieval; also of Yorkshire.
See also Eskelby

Exley

EXLEY, VICTOR. 'The Exley family of Rawdon', *B.A.* 12; N.S. 10(47), 1982, 87-97. 16-20th c.

EXLEY, VIC. 'The Exleys: a genealogical study', *O.W.R.* 3(2), 1983, 32-3. 14-18th c.

Eyre

HULBERT, M.F.H. *Legends of the Eyres (fact and fiction).* Hathersage: Hathersage Parochial Church Council, 1981. Brief; includes pedigree, undated.

Fairbanks

FAIRBANKS, HIRAM FRANCIS. 'Fairbanks marriages in the parish of Halifax, West Riding of Yorkshire', *New England historical and genealogical register* 60 1906, 152-4. 16-17th c.

Fairburn

'The Fairburn thicket', *Y.F.H.* 14(6), 1988, 149-51. Includes pedigree, 17-19th c.

Fairfax

AVELING, HUGH. 'The Catholic recusancy of the Yorkshire Fairfaxes', *Biographical studies* 3, 1955-6, 69-114; *Recusant history* 4, 1957-8, 61-101; 6 1961-2, 12-54 & 95-111. 16-19th c., includes list of chaplains.

BAILDON, W. PALEY. 'Acaster Malbis and the Fairfax family', *Y.A.J.* 19, 1906-7, 19-30. Includes medieval pedigrees.

HARRISON, C.C. 'The Fairfax family', *Old Yorkshire* 8, 1891, 196-202. 15-18th c.

HUNTLEY, LOCKWOOD. *The Fairfaxes of Denton and of Nun Appleton.* York: Yorkshire Gazette, 1905. Pamphlet, medieval-17th c.

TENISON, C.M. 'Fairfax', *M.G.H.* 4th series **2**, 1908, 65. 18th c. No location given, but presumably related to the Yorkshire family.

WADDINGTON, G.W. 'The Fairfax family: extracts from the parish registers of Whitby, Co. York', *Genealogist* 2, 1878, 390.

Farrer

BRETTON, R. 'A recorded pedigree of the Farrers of Ewood', *T.Hal.A.S.* 1939, 161-207. 16-18th c.

FARRER, LILIAN K.P. 'The English ancestry of Jacob Farrer of Lancaster, Mass', *New England historical and genealogical register* **95**, 1941, 1-13. Includes folded pedigree of Farrer of Halifax, 16-17th c.

FARRER, THOMAS CECIL, LORD. *Some Farrer memorials, being a selection from the papers of Thomas Henry, first Lord Farrer, 1819-1899, on various matters connected with his life, with notes relating to some branches of the family of Greystoneley, Ingleborough, Abinger, between 1616 and 1923.* George Sherwood, 1923. Includes pedigrees, 17-20th c.

WEBSTER, C.D. 'A Farrer descent', *T.Hal.A.S.* 1968, 37-43. 17-18th c.

'Farrer of Ewood, Co. York, Hoddesdon, Co. Herts., and Croxton, Co. Lincs,' *M.G.H.* 5th series **9**, 1935-7, 224-8. Pedigree, 16-18th c., includes will of Montague Farrer of Port Royal, Jamaica, 1680.

Fawcett

SCRUTON, WILLIAM. 'The Fawcett family', *Y.N.Q.II.* 4, 1908, 194-200. See also 220. 18-19th c.

'Dr Fawcett and his times', *Y.N.Q.II.* 1, 1905, 247-52. Includes pedigree, 18-19th c.

'Pedigree of the Fawcetts of Bradford', *Y.N.Q.II.* 4, 1908, 228-9. 18-19th c.

Fawsitt

See Ferguson

Fawkes

DAVIES, ROBERT. *The Fawkes's of York in the sixteenth century, including notices of the early history of Guye Fawkes, the Gunpowder plot conspirator.* J.B. Nichols & J.G.Nichols, 1850. 16-17th c.

SHARPLES, MARION. *The Fawkes family and their estates in Wharfedale, 1819-1936.* T.S. 2nd series **6**. 1997. Based on an M.Phil thesis; includes pedigree.

SHARPLES, M. 'The Fawkes-Turner connection, and the art at Farnley Hall, Otley, 1792-1937: a great estate enhanced and supported', *N.H.* **26**, 1990, 131-59.

Fearnley
See Whitaker

Featherby
FEATHERBY, WILLIAM. *A Yorkshire furrow: the story of the Featherbys.* Old Woking: Unwin Brothers, 1993. 12-20th c.

Fenton
GOODCHILD, JOHN. *The coal kings of Wakefield.* Wakefield Historical Publications, 1978. Fenton and Charlesworth families, c.1750-1900.

Ferguson
LYTHE, S.G.E. *Two families of Walkington (1808-1933).* Glasgow: Polpress, 1992. Ferguson and Fawsitt families.

Ferrand
C., J.A. 'The Ferrand pedigree', *Y.G.* **2**, 1890, 29-30. Includes brief pedigree, 18-19th c.
'Ferrand', *Y.G.* **1**, 1888, 240-42. 16-17th c.

Ffarington
See Way

Field
FIELD, OSGOOD. *The Field's of Sowerby, near Halifax, England and of Flushing, New York, with some notices of the families of Underhill, Bowne, Burling, Hazard and Osgood.* Privately published, 1895. Includes pedigrees, 13-19th c.

FIELD, OSGOOD. 'Notes upon the Field family', *New England historical and genealogical register* **22**, 1868, 166-73. Includes pedigree of Field of East Ardsley, 16-17th c.

FIELD, OSGOOD. 'Sketch of the family of Field, of the West Riding of Yorkshire, England, and of Flushing and Newtown, Long Island, New York', *New England historical and genealogical register* **17**, 1863, 106-12. Medieval-19th c.
See also Wilmer

Fielden
FISHWICK, HENRY. *A genealogical memorial of the family of Fielden of Todmorden, in the counties of York and Lancaster, with appendices of parish registers, wills, monumental inscriptions, and original documents, together with notices of the family in Newark, in the county of Nottingham, and in various parts of Lancashire and Yorkshire.* Mitchell and Hughes, 1884. Includes folded pedigree, 16-19th c.

Firth
'Quaker families: Firth pedigree', *Y.C.M.* **1**, 1891, 289-91. 18-19th c.
See also Hall

Fisher
FISHER, WILLIAM SCOTT. 'The Catholic Fishers of Yarm, North Riding of Yorkshire', *Catholic ancestor* **6**(2), 1996, 69-75. 18th c.

MYERSCOUGH, CORITA. 'The Fishers of York: a family of sculptors', *York historian* **7**, 1986, 46-59. Includes pedigree, 19th c.

Fitzalan
CLAY, C.T. 'Notes on the origin of the Fitzalans of Bedale', *Y.A.J.* **30**, 1931, 281-90. Medieval, includes pedigrees, 12-13th c.

Fitzhugh
See Hassard

Fitzwilliam
DUCKHAM, B.F. 'The Fitzwilliams and the navigation of the Yorkshire Derwent', *N.H.* **2**, 1967, 45-61. 18-19th c.

MEE, G. *Aristocratic enterprise: the Fitzwilliam industrial enterprise.* Glasgow: Blackie, 1975. Includes chapter on 'the owners of Wentworth Woodhouse', i.e. the Fitzwilliam family.

Fleck
See Cook

Flemyng
'Flemyngs of Dalton, Huddersfield', *Y.C.M.* **3**, 1893, 151, 14-15th c.

Foggitt

FOGGIT, PAUL. 'The Foggitt family of Aireborough', *Wh N.* **18,** 1995, 18-19. 19th c.

Forster

FOSTER, JOSEPH. *A pedigree of the Forsters and Fosters of the north of England, and of some of the families connected with them.* Privately published, 1871. Detailed; includes pedigrees, medieval-19th c.

WARWICK, MARGARET, & WARWICK, DENNIS. *The Forsters of Burley-in-Wharfedale.* Burley in Wharfedale: Burley in Wharfedale Local History Group Publications, 1994. 19th c.

Forz
See Eston

Foster

BARRETT, F. 'The Fosters of Black Dyke Mills', *T.Hal.A.S.* 1967, 55-72. 19-20th c.

BROOK, FLORENCE FOSTER. *Beckermonds in Langstrothdale.* Ripon: the author, 1962. Foster family; includes pedigree, 18-20th c.

FOSTER, FLORENCE. 'Beckermonds in Langstrothdale', *Dalesman* **10,** 1948, 11-15, 67-9, 93-5 & 132-5. Foster family, 18th c.

See also Forster

Fothergill

FOTHERGILL, RICHARD. *The Fothergills: a first history.* Privately published, 1999. Not seen. Of Ravenstonedale and Mallerstang, Westmorland, and Yorkshire.

'Marriage certificate, 1673: Fothergill of Wensleydale', *Friends Historical Society journal* **33,** 1937, 68-9. Certificate of the Quaker marriage of Alexander Fothergill and Ann Langton, with list of 18 witnesses,

Foulds

FOULDS, STUART. 'An interesting Foulds family with Sheffield associations', *F.S.* **9**(3), 1989, 66-7. 18-19th c.

Fountayne

MURRAY, HUGH. 'Rainwater heads and fall pipe brackets', *Y.A.S., F.H.P.S.S.N.* 4(5), 1978, 171-2. Fountayne family; includes pedigree, 18-19th c.

Fowler

LANE, MICHAEL R. *The story of the steam plough works: Fowlers of Leeds.* Northgate Publishing, 1980. Primarily a history of the business, but includes pedigree of Fowler, 18-19th c.

Foxcroft
See Henrison

Franks

FRANK, BERT. 'The Franks: a yeoman family of Hutton-le-Hole', *Ryedale historian* **13,** 1986, 73-8; **14,** 1988-9, 42-50. Medieval-19th c.

See also Hall

Frend
See Blackburne

Frobisher

FROBISHER, GEORGE. 'The Frobishers of the North West Company', *O.W.R.* 4(2), 1984, 1-3. 18th c.

Fryer

CLAY, H. TRAVIS. 'The Fryers of Rastrick', *T.Hal.A.S.* 1951, 63-70. Includes folded pedigree, 18-19th c.

'Quaker families: Fryer pedigree', *Y.C.M.* **1,** 1891, 292. Of Toothill, 19th c.

Fulwood
See Lewen

Furniss

SMITH, BARBARA M. 'A yeoman family: Furniss of Hathersage and Sheffield', *E.C.A. [English catholic ancestor] journal* 2(7), 1989, 154-7. See also inside back cover. Includes pedigree, 17-20th c., showing connection with Collins.

Gale
See Stukeley

Galliard
See Vescy

Garford/th
GARFORD, JOHN. 'Garford of Steeton Hall, Yorkshire, and Garford of Corby, Lincolnshire: Arthur Garforth, afterwards called Garford', *Northern genealogist* **4**, 1901, 137. 17th c.
MURRAY, HUGH. 'Rainwater heads and fallpipe brackets, part 2', *Y.A.S., F.H.P.S.S.N.* 4(6), 1978, 186-7. Garforth family; includes pedigree. 18th c.

Gargrave
'The pedigree of the family of Gargrave', *M.G.H.* **1**, 1868, 226-7. Medieval-17th c.

Gartside
WRIGHT, A.E.G. 'The Gartsides of Woodbrow', *B.S.H.S.* 22(1), 1992, 8-10. 19th c.

Gascoigne
HUNTLEY, LOCKWOOD. *The Gascoignes of Harewood.* Historic Yorkshire families series 12. York: North of England Newspaper Co., 1906. Reprinted from the *Yorkshire gazette.*
ROSS, F. 'The Gascoigne family', *Old Yorkshire* **2**, 1881, 162-5. Medieval-19th c.

Garrett
see Leckey

Gatenby
KEMP, IVY MARGARET 'Twenty generations of Gatenbys at Chapel Garth Farm, Ripon', *R.H.* 4(1), 1999, 11-14. Includes pedigree from the visitation return of 1575.
'The Gatenbys of Helperby', *C.Y.D.F.H.S.N.* **23**, 1991, 14-16. Includes pedigree, 17-19th c.

Gavin
See Cutsforth

Geldart
See Gildart

Gell
'The family of Gell', *B.T.* **6**, 1980, 11-12. Brief note.

Gibson
RUSBY, JAMES. 'The family of Gibson', *Y.G.* **1**, 1888, 78-84. Mainly extracts from parish registers, marriage licences, monumental inscriptions, *etc.,* 17-18th c.

Gilbert
See Royds

Gildart
GILDART, CHARLES R. *The Gildart-Geldart families.* [Sierra Madre, California]: privately published, 1962. Of Carlton, Yorkshire, Liverpool, Staffordshire and the United States, 17-20th c.

Gill
See Coates

Girlington
R., J. 'Pedigree of Girlington, of Girlington Hall in the parish of Wycliffe, in Richmondshire and North Riding of the county of York', *Collectanea topographica et genealogica* **6**, 1840, 190-91. 13-17th c.

Gledhill
COX, SHEILA. 'The Gledhill family of Yorkshire, Norfolk, and Kansas, U.S.A.', *B.A.* 3rd series **5**, 1991, 68-71. 19-20th c.
KENDAL, HUGH P. 'Barkisland Hall and the family of Gledhill', *P.R.H.A.S.* 1922, 105-23. 16-17th c.

Glover
GLOVER, THOMAS C. *Sex and violence in the Vale of York: a history of the Glover family and their forebears.* 2nd ed. [Bedale]: the authors, 1990. Includes pedigree, 18-20th c.

Goldesborough
GOLDSBROUGH, ALBERT. *Memorials of the Goldesborough family.* Cheltenham: E.J. Burrow & Co., 1930. Of Yorkshire and various other counties, medieval-19th c., includes pedigrees.

Goodricke
History of the Goodricke family. Rev. ed. [ ], 1897. Medieval-19th c., includes many extracts from original sources.

Gorrell

POSTLETHWAITE, REG. 'The mystery of the Gorrells of Chapel House Farm, Dalehead, Slaidburn', *Y.F.H.* 20(6), 1994, 150-6. Includes pedigree, 17-20th c.

Gosling

'Gosling of Stubley and Sheffield', *T.Hunter A.S.* 4, 1937, 143-4. Includes folded pedigree, 17-18th c.

Gott

BUTTERWORTH, PATRICIA C. 'The Gotts of Bingley and Gotts Yard', *K.D.F.H.S.J.* Spring 1992, 17-19.

BUTTERWORTH, TRICIA, & BUTTERWORTH, ROY. 'Gott's Yard: the story of a Bingley family', *Y.F.H.* 19(6), 1993, 126-7. 18-20th c.

DAVIES, ERNEST. 'Gotts of Bingley and Gotts Yard: a further contribution', *K.D.F.H.S.J.* Spring 1994, 6-8. 19-20th c.

'Gott of Calverley', *Y.C.M.* 3, 1893, 112. Pedigree, 17-18th c.

Graham

MACKEAN, W.H. *The Grahams of Kirkstall.* [H.F.Graham], [1960?] 18-20th c.

Gray

COBB, WILLIAM. *A history of the Grays of York, 1695-1988.* York, William Sessions, 1989. Includes pedigrees of Gray, 18-20th c., Dodsworth, 18-20th c. and Elmhirst, 19-20th c.

GRAY, A. *Papers and diaries of a York family, 1764-1839.* Sheldon Press, 1927. Gray family, 18-19th c.

See also Cutsforth

Grayson

See Bedford

Green(e)

LANCASTER, W.T. 'The family of Green of Horsforth', in *Miscellanea* [7]. *T.S.* 24, 1919 469-70. Brief note, 16th c.

'The Greene family of Liversedge', *Old Yorkshire* 4, 1883, 221-232. 13-19th c.

'Notes relating to the families of Green and Armitage from the collections of Mr. William Radclyffe, Rouge Croix', *M.G.H.* N.S., 3, 1880, 122-3. 18th c.

See also Brewster and Wilmer

Greenroyd

(See Ackroyd

Greenwood

KENDALL, HUGH P. 'Learings in Heptonstall', *P.R.H.A.S.* 1919, 49-63. Greenwood family, 16th c.

RILEY, PHILIP E. 'The Greenwood's story', *B.T.* 26, 1986, 11-14. Originally of Malton; also of London, Pembroke, *etc.*

Grene

See Brewster

Gresham

See Thwaytes

Grice

ROWE, J. 'Grice family history', *Wakefield & District F.H.S. Journal* 2(1), 1998, 23-6. 14-17th c.

Grimshaw

BAKER, F. 'The Grimshaw family', *T.Hal.A.S.* 1945, 49-72. 17-19th c.

See also Skeet

Grimston

INGRAM, M. EDWARD. *Leaves from a family tree, being the correspondence of an East Riding family.* Hull: A. Brown & Sons, 1951. Grimston family history, 18-19th c., of Goodmanthorpe.

KING, NORAH. *The Grimstons of Gorhambury.* Chichester: Phillimore, 1983. Originally of Yorkshire.

MOOR, C. 'The early Grimstons', *Genealogist* N.S., 29, 1913, 129-44. 13-15th c.

See also Legard

Gulson/Gulston

See Smith

Gyles

BRIGHTON, JT. *Henry Gyles, virtuoso and glasspainter of York, 1645-1709.* York historian 4. 1984. Includes pedigree, 16-17th c.

Habishaw

See Coates

Hagen

See Smith

Haggerston

'Haggerston pedigree', *Y.G.* **2**, 1890, 129-30. 17-19th c.

Haigh

PATTISON, T. 'Relations, friends & acquaintances of Robert Hargreaves Haigh', *K.D.F.H.S.J.* Autumn 1998, 6-9. Mainly notes on the Haigh and Hargreaves families, 19th c

Haldenby

TENISON, C.M. 'Pedigree of Haldenby of Haldenby, Yorkshire', *M.G.H.* 4th series **4**, 1911, 71-4. 16-17th c.

Hall

BROOKE, SUSAN. 'Some notes on the Hall family of Stumperlow and Leeds', in *Thoresby miscellany* **12**. *T.S.* **41**. 1954, 309-51. 18-19th c., includes pedigrees showing connection of Hall, Clayton, Spencer, Broadbent, Smeaton and Clapham.

'Hall pedigree', *Y.G.* **2**, 1890, 187-90. See also 246. 17-18th c., showing descent through Firth, Franks and Walker, *etc.*

Halstead

See Mitchell

Hands

See Dale

Hansome

See Hanson

Hanson

ARMYTAGE, G.J. 'Ancient pedigree of the Hanson family', *Y.A.J.* 1(1), 1870, 79-85. Medieval-17th c., of Raistrick, Woodhouse, *etc.*

CLAY, H.T. 'Upper and Lower Woodhouse, Rastrick', *T.Hal.A.S.* 1950, 63-6. Hanson family, 14-17th c.

HANSOM, JOSEPH. 'The roll of the freemen of York, and a pedigree of Hanson or Hansome', *Northern genealogist* **6**, 1903, 14-15. 16-18th c.

HULBERT, CANON. 'Hanson family: extracts from the register of the parish church of Almondbury, Yorkshire', *M.G.H.* 5th series **1**, 1916, 246. 16-17th c.

ORMEROD, HANSON. *The pedigree of Hanson of Woodhouse & Hoyle of Swift-Place, Co. York.* Oxford: B.H. Blackwell, 1916. Includes pedigrees, 13-19th c., many wills, extracts from parish registers, *etc.*

REDMONDS, GEORGE. 'Surname history: Hanson', *H. & D.F.H.S.J.* 1(3), 1988, 67.

'A 16th century manuscript relating to the Hanson family of Woodhouse in Raistrick', *B.A.* **8**; N.S. **6**, 1940, 24.

'Hanson pedigree', *Y.G.* **1**, 1888, 86-91, 156-63, 201 & 214. Medieval-19th c.

See also Levett

Harbottle

See Leckey

Hardisty

DAWSON, JOANNA. 'The Hardisty family of Hardisty Hall', *Wh.N.* **21**, 1996, 22-3. Medieval-19th c., brief.

Hargrave

SAMUEL, R. 'My grandfather was a harbourmaster', *Y.F.H.* 16(6), 1990, 150-52. Hargrave family of Knottingley; includes pedigree, 19-20th c.

Hargreaves

SINNOTT, K. 'Pedigree of Hargreaves', *K.D.F.H.S.J.* Winter 1996, 14-15. 18-20th c.

See also Haigh

Harling

EASTWOOD, DAVID. 'Lieutenant Edward Harling of Almondbury', *Y.F.H.* 21(3), 1995, 62-6; 21(4), 1995, 99-104. Harling family, 18th c.

Harris

SPERRY, KIP. 'Margaret Harris of Boston, Massachusetts, and Yorkshire, England', *New England historical and genealogical register* **140**, 1986, 63-4. 18th c.

Harrison

HARRISON, BILL. *The Harrisons of Gisburn Forest: a register of the descendants of Stephen Harrison (1685-1747).* Settle: Owlshaw Books, 1995. Originally of Bolland.

HORNSEY, MARGARET. 'John Harrison, the Leeds benefactor, and his times', in *Miscellanea* [10]. *T.S.* **33**, 1935, 103-47. Includes pedigree, 17th c.

LUMB, G.D. 'The family of John Harrison, the Leeds benefactor', in *Miscellanea* [5]. *T.S.* **15**, 1909, 48-55. Includes wills of John Harrison, 1601, Thomas Foxcroft, 1596, and John Henrison, 1553.

MORTON, A.L. 'The hero as genealogist: General Plantagenet-Harrison', *Y.A.J.* **40**, 1962, 351-70. Primarily a biography of an eccentric genealogist, but includes notes on the Harrison family, 18-19th c.

ROBINSON, W. GORDON. 'The Harrisons of Skipton', *Congregational Historical Society transactions* **20**, 1970, 322-33. Includes pedigree, 18-19th c.

'Harrison, of Whitgift in the West Riding of Yorkshire, and North Place, Co. Lincoln', *M.G.H.* 5th series **3**, 1918-19, 21-2. 16-19th c.

See also Smith

Hartley
'More Bowland families', *Y.F.H.* **21**(1), 1995, 5-6. See also **21**(4), 1995, 104-5. Hartley and Capstick families, 18-19th c.

Harwood
HARWOOD, H.W. 'A family of smiths', *T.Hal.A.S.* 1961, 17-22. Harwood family, 17-20th c.

Hassard
SHORT, H.HASSARD. *Outline of the history and genealogy of the Hassards and their connections.* York: H.Sotheran, 1858. Of various counties, including Yorkshire; medieval-19th c. Also includes pedigrees of allied families — Short of Doncaster, Armitage of Doncaster, Longe of Clerkenwell, Fitzhugh, Lamplugh of Lamplugh, Cumberland, *etc.*

Hastings
See Wheler

Havelock
'Notes on families bearing the surname Havelock', *Northern genealogist* **4**, 1901, 150-3. Of Yorkshire and Essex; includes wills.

Haw
See Coates

Hawke
'Records of a Hawke family of the Bradfield area', *F.S.* **11**(1), 1990, 23. From an old family bible, 19th c.

Hawksworth
HAWKSWORTH, J.M. 'Some Hawksworths in the Bradfield area', *F.S.* **5**(2), 1984, 43-4. 19th c.

Haworth
HAWORTH-BOOB, B.B. 'Haworth or Howarth pedigree', *M.G.H.* N.S., **1** 1874, 57-8. Of Snaith, 16-18th c.

Haythorn(e)
COLLINS, DOROTHY HAYTHORN H. *The Haythorn(e)s: a history and genealogy.* [ ]: L.P. Thebault Company, 1982. Of Yorkshire, Lancashire and the United States.

Hazard
See Field

Heape
HEAPE, CHARLES, & HEAPE, RICHARD. *Records of the family of Heape of Heape, Staley, Saddleworth, and Rochdale, from circa 1170 to 1905.* Rochdale: Aldine Press, 1905. Includes pedigrees (some folded), and many extracts from original sources.

Heaton
EDGERLEY, MABEL C. 'Ponden Hall and the Heatons', *Brontë Society transactions* **10**(6), 1945, 265-8. 16-18th c.

HOLMES, HAZEL. 'The Heaton family', *K.D.F.H.S.J.* Summer 1991, 9-12. Of Ponden, *etc.*, includes pedigree, medieval-19th c.

Hedley
See Smith

Heeley
REDMONDS, GEORGE. 'Surname history: Heeley', *H. & D.F.H.S.J.* **7**(4), 1994, 139. Discussion of the surname.

Heblethwayte
BROWNE, G. OSBORNE. 'Heblethwayte
pedigree', *M.G.H.* N.S., **1**, 418-9. 16-19th c.

Heginbottom
See Eastwood

Hellawell
REDMONDS, GEORGE. 'Surname history:
Hellawell', *H. & D.F.H.S.J.* 4(2), 1991, 71.

Hemingway
LISTER, JOHN. 'Over Brea & Nether Brea: the
Hemingway family', *P.R.H.A.S.* 1917, 89-111.
16-17th c.
REDMONDS, GEORGE. 'English origins:
Hemingway', *Nexus: the bimonthly
newsletter of the New England Historic
Genealogy Society* 5(3)) 1988, 99-100. 14-
16th c., notes on distribution of the
surname in Yorkshire.

Hemsworth
HEALD, GEOFFREY. 'Danish treasure trail',
Don. Anc. 2(4), 1984, 108-9. Hemsworth
family, medieval-17th c.
HIMSWORTH, J.B. 'Gabriel Hemsworth (or
Himsworth) (Sheffield Castle, 1644) and
his family in Yorkshire', *T.Hunter A.S.* **6**,
1950, 310-13. 17-18th c.

Henderson
BENTON, JOAN, & ELMER, SHEILA.
'Serendipity', *C.Y.D.F.H.S.J.* **43**, 1997, 8-10.
Henderson and Reynoldson families, 18th c.

Herbert
DAVIES, ROBERT. 'A memoir of Sir Thomas
Herbert, of Tinterne, in the County of
Monmouth, and of the City of York,
Baronet', *Y.A.J.* **1**, 1870, 182-214. Includes
folded pedigree, 15-17th c.
HUNTLEY, LOCKWOOD. *The Herberts of
York*. Historic Yorkshire families series **8**.
York: North of England Newspaper Co.,
1905. Reprinted from the *Yorkshire
gazette.*
See also Wilmer

Hey
REDMONDS, GEORGE. 'Surname history: Hey',
H. & D.F.H.S.J. 3(2), 1990, 53.

Hibbe(r)s(t)on(e)
'Surname variations', *F.S.* 10(3), 1990, 63-4.
Hibberston/Ibbutson family of Gringley on
the Hill, Nottinghamshire, and Sheffield.
18-19th c.

Hibbert
BOULTER, W. CONSITT. 'Hibbert', *M.G.H.* N.S.,
1, 1974, 367. Of Preston, late 17th c.

Hickham
See Coates

Higgins
See Hill

Hildyard
CROUCH, CHAS. HALL. 'The Hildyards of
Winestead', *Y.N.Q.II.* **5**, 1909, 83-5.
Medieval-18th c.
ROSS, F. 'The Hildyards of Winestead in
Holderness', *Old Yorkshire* **4**, 1883, 232-9.
Medieval-17th c.
See also Legard

Hilileigh
R., F. 'Hilileigh or Hillilee familiy', *Northern
genealogist* **5**, 1902, 75-6. Extracts from
Halifax parish register.

Hill
'The Hill and the Higgins families', *B.A.* **7**;
N.S., **5**, 1933, 188. Compiled from parish
registers of Carlton, Bradford, *etc.*
See also Way

Hillilee
See Hilileigh

Hilton
GIBSON, DENNY. 'The story behind the stone:
a Dalesman who declined God's Acre',
J.Cl.F.H.S. 5(8), 1993, 41-5. Hilton family
of Cotherstone, 19-20th c.

Himsworth
See Hemsworth

Hinchcliff
BRADLEY, A.C. 'The land tax and Joseph
Hinchcliff', *H. & D.F.H.S.J.* 5(4), 1992,
118-9. Early 19th c.

Hinchliff

COLLINS, EWEN. 'Family Bible jottings', *H. & D.F.H.S.J.* **8**,(1), 1994, 27-8. Hinchliff family, 19th c.

Hirst

'A Primitive Methodist ministerial romance: the Hirst family', *Wesley Historical Society (Yorkshire Branch) [newsletter]* **71**, 1997, 2-8.
See also Peirse

Hoby

See Danby and Legard

Hodgson

HODGSON, GEOFFREY MARTIN. *A Hodgson family.* Standon, Herts.: the author, 1982. Includes pedigree, 17-20th c.
HODGSON, GORDON. 'The Hodgsons of Scholes and Bradford', *Y.F.H.* **13**(5), 1987, 97-8. Brief discussion.
M., J.E. 'William Hodgson's book', *Thoresby miscellany* **13**. T.S. **46**, 1963, 379-80. Brief note on manuscript notes concerning the Hodgson family *etc.*
See also Benson

Holder

HOLDER, CHARLES FREDERICK. *The Holders of Holderness: a history and genealogy of the Holder family, with especial reference to Christopher Holder, head of the American Quaker branch ...* [Pasadena]: [ ], 1902. Not seen.

Holland

HOLLAND, JOHN. 'The late Samuel Holland of Sheffield', *Reliquary* **11**, 1870-71, 13-16. Includes pedigree, 18-19th c.

Holmes

ADRIAN, RICHARD H. 'A very interesting note', *K.D.F.H.S.J.* Autumn 1993, 18-20. Includes pedigree of Holmes and Lambert families, 18-20th c.
COE, SHEILA. 'My Holmes connections', *Wh.N.* **13**, 1994, 10-12. 17-18th c.
HOLMES, PETER. 'A Bradford department store and its Victorian founders', *Y.A.J.* **70**, 1998, 141-56. Holmes family.
'Pedigree of Holmes', *K.D.F.H.S.J.* Summer 1995, 14-15. 18-20th c.

Holroyd(e)

WRIGHT, H. 'Some of our local people named Holroyde', *T.Hal.A.S.* 1932, 93-127. 17-19th c.
See also Ackroyd

Hoole

DRURY, CHARLES. 'John Hook', *T.Hunter A.S.* **2**(2), 1921, 204. Pedigree of Hoole of Sheffield, 17-19th c.
ADDY, S.O. 'The Hoole family of Sheffield and the Sandersons', *T.Hunter A.S.* **3**, 1929, 215-23. Includes will of Robert Saunderson of Blythe Abbey, Nottinghamshire, 1608.
DRURY, CHARLES. 'John Hoole', *Notes & queries* 12th series **8**, 1919, 327. See also 8th series **9**, 307 & 518. Pedigree of Hoole of Sheffield, 17-19th c.

Hooper

See Rawlins

Hopkinson

BROWN, JEAN K. 'Hopkinsonne Farm', *Bod-Kin* **2**(7) 1998, 7-9; **2**(8), 1998, 16-19. At Thornton; Hopkinson family, 17-19th c.

Hopton

TAYLOR, R.V. 'The Hoptons of Armley', *Old Yorkshire* **2**, 1881, 160-62. 16-18th c.

Horbury

CLAY, C.T. 'Notes on the early generations of the family of Horbury', *Y.A.J.* **26**, 1922, 334-45. Includes pedigree, 12-13th c.

Horne

HORNE, J FLETCHER. 'The Hornes of Mexborough', *Y.A.J.* **19**, 1906-7, 417-34. Includes pedigree, 16-18th c.

Horner

'A Hull connection' *R.H.* **3**(1), 1996, 9-12. Horner family of Nidderdale and Hull; includes pedigree, 17-19th c.

Hornshaw

WOOD, JOHN EDWIN. *The Hornshaws of Thorp Arch, Yorkshire.* Havant: J.E.Wood, 1994. Includes pedigree, 19-20th c.

Horsfall

T[URNER], J.H. 'The Horsfall family', *Y.C.M.* **4**, 1894, 201-11. Medieval-16th c.

'Horsfall families', *Y.G.* **2**, 1890, 294-5. 18-19th c.

Horsman

HORSMAN, ERIC M. 'My successful search for ancestors (or, perseverance rewarded at last)', *Y.A.S., F.H.P.S.S.N.* 7(1), 1981, 95-8.

Horton

KENDALL, H.P. 'Sowerby Hall', *P.R.H.A.S.* 1910, 169-200. Account of its associations, especially with the Horton family, 17-18th c.

LINTON, EDWARD F. *The Hortons of Howroyde and some allied families. I. Horton, II. Linton. III. Richardson.* Cambridge: J. Webb & Co., 1911. Medieval-19th c. Linton of Freiston and Stirtloe, Huntingdonshire, Richardson of St Bees, Cumberland, and York.

Hotham

SALTMARSHE, PHILIP. *History and chartulary of the Hothams of Scorborough in the East Riding of Yorkshire, 1100-1700.* York: Ben Johnson & Company, 1914. Includes pedigrees, but *not,* strictly speaking, a chartulary.

STIRLING, A.M.W. *The Hothams: being the chronicles of the Hothams of Scorborough and South Dalton from their hitherto unpublished family papers.* 2 vols. Herbert Jenkins, 1918. 14-19th c.

See also Legard

Howard

The house of Howard and Sheffield: their connections, 1606-1917. Local history leaflets 9. Sheffield: Sheffield City Libraries, 1960. Brief, includes pedigree.

Howorth

See Haworth

Hoyle

HOYLE, PERCY SAVILE. 'Hoyle', *Y.G.* **2**, 1890, 40-42. Includes pedigrees, 16-19th c.

'Hoyle of Light Hazels, in the Graveship of Sowerby, parish of Halifax, county York', *Y.G.* **1**, 1888, 190-91. Pedigree, 16-17th c.

See also Hanson

Hucks

See Barnett

Huddleston

HUDDLESTON, W. 'The Huddleston family', *J.Cl.F.H.S.* 1(1), 1980, 11-15. Medieval-18th c.

Hudson

See Royd(s)

Hullah / Hulley

HULLAH, S.C. 'A family in 18th century Leeds', *Y.F.H.* **20**(2), 1994, 44-6. Hullah or Hulley family.

HULLEY, GERALD F. *The Hulleys of Yorkshire.* Privately published, 1992. 16-20th c. Includes pedigree.

HULLAH, SHEILA C. 'Hullah or Hulley?' *Y.F.H.* **15**(3), 1989, 80-82. 18-19th c.

Humble

RAE, PAMELA. *Turtle at Mr. Humble's: the fortunes of a mercantile family, England & America, 1758-1837.* Otley: Smith Settle, 1992. Of Bradford. Includes folded pedigree of the Dawson, Buck and Whittaker families, 18th c.

Huntington

See Munkton

Hunton

KAYE, WALTER J. 'Anthony Hunton, M.D., an Elizabethan physician, and his connexion with Harrogate', in *Miscellanea* [9]. *T.S.* **28**, 1928, 212-25. Includes wills of Anthony Hunton, 1624, and of Mordecai Hunton, 1638.

Hurt

SITWELL, GEORGE RERESBY, SIR. *The Hurts of Haldworth and their descendents at Savile Hall, The Ickles, and Hesley Hall, being a study of social and domestic life in past times, more particularly in Hallamshire and at Nottingham during the reign of Elizabeth, at Rotherham under Cromwell, and at Sheffield in the eighteenth century.* Oxford: Oxford University Press, 1930, Includes pedigrees.

Huscroft

HUSCROFT, ARTHUR. 'Early instances of the name Huscroft', *Don. Anc.* 1(3), 1981, 101-4. Medieval-17th c.

Hussey

See Roberts

Hustler

B[RUCE], W.D. 'Hustler of Acklam in Cleveland', *Topographer & genealogist* **1**, 1846, 497-9.

MAFFEY, JOHN. 'On some of the decayed families of Bradford', *B.A.* **1**, 1888, 26-32. Hustler family; includes pedigree, 18-19th c.

Hutchinson

CHESTER, JOSEPH LEMUEL. *A genealogy of the Hutchinson family of Yorkshire, and of the American branch of the family descended from Richard Hutchinson of Salem, Mass.* Boston: D. Clapp & Son, 1868. Reprinted from *New England historical and genealogical register.*

DERBY, PERLEY. *The Hutchinson family, or, the descendants of Barnard Hutchinson of Cowlam, England.* Salem: Essex Institute Press, 1870. Not seen.

Hutton

BRAYSHAY, WILLIAM HUTTON. 'The Hutton family', *Old Yorkshire* **1**, 1881, 220-25. 16-17th c.

WHEATCROFT, W. 'The silversmith Huttons of Sheffield', *F.S.* **7**(4), 1987, 98-9. 18-20th c.

WHITING, C.E. 'The Huttons of Hooton Pagnell', *T.Hunter A.S.* **6**, 1950, 25-37. 17-18th c.

I'Anson

I'ANSON, WILLIAM. 'The Lass of Richmond Hill', *Y.A.J.* **25**, 1908-9, 101-3. I'Anson family, 17-18th c.

Ibbetson / Ibbotson

FUREY, MARGARET. 'The Ibbotsons of Wortley in the 18th and early 19th centuries', *F.S.* **16**(1), 1995, 23-40.

RODGER, MARGERY. 'Ibbotson of Hathersage', *F.S.* **1** (4), 1978, 86-90. Family wills, 17-18th c.

WILSON, R.G. 'Merchants and land: the Ibbetsons of Leeds and Denton, 1650-1850', **24**, 1988, 75-100.
See also Hibbe(r)s(t)on(e)

Ingham

See Whitaker

Ingilby

LANCASTER, W.T. *The early history of Ripley and the Ingilby family, with some account of the Roos family of Ingmanthorpe.* Leeds: John Whitehead & Son, 1918. Medieval; includes pedigrees and deed abstracts.

Insula de Rubeo Monte

DUCKETT, GEORGE, SIR. 'Robert de Insula de Rubeo Monte (Harwood evidences)', *Y.A.J.* **4**, 1877, 107-13. Includes medieval pedigree.

Ingram

Temple Newsam House. Leeds: Leeds Corporation Libraries & Arts Committee, 1951. Includes account of the Ingram family.

Issott

'An eighteenth century absolution', *Y.A.J.* **16**, 1900-1901, 256-7. Of William Issott of Horbury; includes Issott family pedigrees.

Jackson

LUMB, G.D. 'The Old Hall, Wade Lane, Leeds, and the Jackson family', in *Miscellanea* **[8]**. *T.S.* **26**, 1924, 1-14. Includes wills, deeds, *etc.,* 16-17th c.
See also Craven

James

CLOUGH, P. 'The ancestry of John James, F.S.A., Bradford historian', *Bod-kin* **15**, 1989, 3-4. 18-19th c.

Jarvis

DAWSON, C.M. 'Jarvis of South Yorkshire', *F.S.* **1**(3), 1978, 64-5. 18-19th c.

Jeans

See Whitaker

Jeffcock

BADGER, FRANCES J. 'The Jeffcocks of Handsworth (or, don't believe official pedigrees)', *F.S.* **5**(3), 1984, 58-62. 18-19th c.

Jefferson

CHRISTIE, BARBARA JEFFERSON. *Sowing the seeds of time: a history of the Jefferson family in the parishes of Lythe and Hinderwell in the North Riding of Yorkshire, 1631-1994.* Issquah, W.A. Jefferson Publishing, 1994. Includes pedigrees.

Jenkins

JACKSON, CHARLES. 'Jenkins', *M.G.H.* N.S., **1**, 1874, 122-3. Pedigree, 16-18th c.

Jenkinson

TINGLE, DEREK. 'Jenkinson: a working class family', *F.S.* **17**(2), 1996, 66-8; **17**(3), 1996, 89-91. Of Ecclesfield and Sheffield, 18-20th c.
See also Coles

Jepson

'A Jepson jaunt', *H. & D.F.H.S.J.* **8**(2), 1995, 55-7. Includes pedigree, 17th c.

Jewett

HAZEN, TRACY ELLIOT. 'Two founders of Rowley, Mass.', *New England historical and genealogical register* **94**, 1940, 99-112. Jewett and Mallinson families of Bradford, 16-17th c., includes wills, parish register extracts, deeds, *etc.*

Jobson

JOBSON, I.M. 'Jobson family', *Notes & queries* **154**, 1928, 119. See also 177 & 250. 16th c., brief.

Johnson

THOMPSON, PISHEY. 'The Johnson family', *New England historical and genealogical register* **8**, 1854, 358-62. Includes pedigree, 16-19th c; of Clipsham, Rutland, Pinchbeck and Spalding, Lincolnshire, Aldborough, Yorkshire, Olney, Buckinghamshire, and Milton Bryant, Bedfordshire.

'Ralph Johnson, vicar of Brignall, 1656-1695', *T.R.S.* **15**, 1945, 9-32. Includes list of Johnson entries from Barningham parish registers, and list of scholars educated under Ralph Johnson at Brignall (from Venn's *Alumni Cantabrigiensis).*
See also Neal

Jones

GREENHOUGH, GEOFFREY. 'My father was a pure Welshman', *Bod-Kin* **20**, 1990, 14-17. Includes pedigree of Jones of Wrexham and Bradford, 18-19th c.

Jowitt

FORSTER, SANDYS B. *The pedigrees of Jowitt, formerly of Churwell, Yorks, and now of Harehills, Leeds.* Privately published, 1890. 18-19th c.

Kaye

KAYE, DONALD. 'Two families from Almondbury', *H. & D.F.H.S.J.* **10**(1), 1996, 25-8. Kaye family, 19-20th c.

Keighley

BAILDON, W. PALEY. 'The Keighley family', *Y.A.J.* **27**, 1924, 1-109. Includes pedigrees, medieval-17th c.

Kendall

ELK-LAND. 'Notes on the family of Kendall, of Yorkshire and Durham', *Y.C.M.* **1**, 1891, 239-44. Includes pedigree, 16-17th c.
See also Robertson

Kenrick
See Way

Kenzie

KENZIE, KEN. 'The game of the name: Kenzie', *Bod-kin* **13**, 1989, 6-9. Of Foulmire, Cambridgeshire, Bradford, *etc.,* 19-20th c.

Ker
See Lewen

Kettlewell

KETTLEWELL, ROBERT. 'Some notes concerning two Yorkshiremen of the revolution', *Y.A.J.* **35**, 1943, 311-20. Kettlewell family, 17th c.

Kilholm / Killam
See Smith

King
EASTWOOD, JAMES. 'The King family',
T.Hal.A.S. 1944, 11-26. 18-19th c.
See also Coates

Kingsley
See Pennyman

Kirby
CURRER-BRIGGS, NOEL. *The search for Mr.
Thomas Kirbye, gentleman.* Chichester:
Phillimore, 1986. Kirby family of Norfolk,
Yorkshire, Hertfordshire, Virginia, *etc.,*
includes pedigrees, 16-20th c.

Kyme
WATSON, G.W. 'The Kymes and their
Parliamentary barony', *M.G.H.* 5th series
8, 1932-4, 65-9. Of Lincolnshire and
Yorkshire, medieval.

La Trobe
'La Trobe', *Y.G.* **2**, 1890, 86-8. Pedigree, 17-
19th c.

Lac(e)y
CLAY, C.T. 'The family of Lacy of
Cromwellbottom and Leventhorpe', in
Miscellanea [9]. *T.S.* **28**, 1928, 48-90.
Medieval-17th c.
DE LACY-BELLENGARI, EDWARD. *The roll of
the Honour of Lacey: pedigrees, military
memoirs and synoptical history of the
ancient and illustrious family of De Lacy
from the earliest times, in all its
branches, to the present day, full notices
on allied families, and a memoir of the
Brownes (Camas).* Baltimore: Waverley
Press, 1928. Actually by Edward Harnett.
Medieval-20th c. Of Pontefract, Ireland,
etc., etc.
NICHOLS, JOHN GOUGH. 'The first and second
houses of Lacy', *Y.A.J.* **2**, 1873, 171-9.
Medieval.
WIGHTMAN, W.E. *The Lacy family in
England and Normandy, 1066-1194.*
Oxford: Clarendon Press, 1966. Includes
pedigrees of the Lacy families of
Pontefract and Herefordshire.

Lambert
ROUND, J. HORACE. 'The tale of a great
forgery', *Ancestor* **3**, 1902, 14-35. Lambert
family of Surrey and Yorkshire, medieval.
See also Holmes

Lamplugh
JABEZ-SMITH, A.R. 'The Lamplughs of
Cockermouth and a Yorkshire inheritance',
*Cumberland and Westmorland
Antiquarian and Archaeological
Association transactions* N.S., **67**, 1967, 81-
92. Includes pedigree, 15-17th c. The
'inheritance' was in Kirby Sigston.
See also Hassard

Langley
'Langley pedigree', *M.G.H.* 2nd series **2**,
1888, 273-83, 305-9 & 337-9; **3**, 1890, 75-80,
141-4, 158-60 & 169-72. Of Shropshire,
Glamorganshire, Warwickshire,
Lancashire, Yorkshire, Kent, and London,
13-19th c.

Langstaff
LONGSTAFF, GEORGE BLUNDELL. *The
Langstaffs of Teesdale and Weardale:
materials for a history of a yeoman
family.* Rev. ed. Mitchell Hughes and
Clarke, 1923. Medieval-20th c., includes
extensive extracts from original sources.

Langton
See Fothergill

Lascelles
'Lascelles of Brakenburgh, Hinderskelfe,
and Eryholme in the County of York',
M.G.H. **2**, 1876, 123-9. Pedigree, medieval-
17th c.

Latham
HORNSBY, JOSEPHINE. 'Some work and family
details of Edward Latham, a 19th c.
Wakefield builder and monumental mason',
Y.A.S., F.H.P.S.S.N. 7(3), 1981, 126-8.

Lawson
ASHCROFT, M.Y. 'The Lawsons of Brough',
Journal **6**, *N.Y.C.R.O.P.* **17**, 1978, 35-45.
Includes summary list of the Lawson of
Brough archive, medieval-19th c.

CLOKIE, SOPHIE P. 'Kirkstall Road Wesleyan Methodist 'iron' chapel, Leeds: the Lawson family and its connections', *Wesley Historical Society (Yorkshire Branch) [newsletter]* **57**, 1990, 7-13. 19th c.
'Lawson, *etc.*,' *Y.C.M.* **1**, 1891, 275. Pedigree, 18th c.
See also Marsden

Laybourn
See Leybourne

Laycock
LAYCOCK, J.A., & LAYCOCK, J.B. 'The Laycocks of the parish of Kildwick', *B.A.* N.S., **3**, 1912, 115-21. Includes folded pedigree, 16-20th c.

Le Roter
HELSBY, T. 'Le Roter or Rutter, of Kingsley, co. Pal. Chester', *Reliquary* **12**, 1871-2, 129-38 & 229-38. Also of New Malton, 16-19th c.

Leach
'Pedigree of the Leaches', *Y.G.* **1**, 1888, 143-50. 15-18th c.

Leadam
'Note on the name of Leadam', *M.G.H.* N.S., **3**, 1880, 182-4. Medieval-18th c.

Leadley
'The Leadley family', *B.T.* **21**, 1985, 23-4. Includes pedigree, 19th c.

Learoyde
See Akroyd

Leather
LEATHER, SIMON R. 'The Leathers in Yorkshire', *Y.F.H.* **16**(3), 1990, 69-72. 18-19th c.

Leathley
BAILDON, W. PAILEY. *The family of Leathley or Lelay.* [The author], [18--]. Abstract from his (then) forthcoming *History of Baildon.* Includes pedigree, 13th c.
BAILDON, W. PALEY. 'The family of Leathley or Lelay', in *Miscellanea* [4]. *T.S.* **11**, 1904, 1-36. Medieval; includes pedigree.

Leavitt
See Levet

Leckey
LECKEY, JOHN. *Leckey and Brammall families.* Toorak, Australia: J.A. Leckey, 1986. Of Scotland, Sheffield, *etc.*, 19-20th c., includes notes, pedigrees, *etc.*, of Chedzoy, Garrett, Harbottle, Oldham and Swellie.

Lee
LEA, J. HENRY. 'Lee of Pocklington', *Genealogist* N.S., **11**, 1895, 203-11. Includes pedigree, 17-18th c., with wills and parish register extracts.
ROBERTS, NANCY V. 'From Sheffield to Queensland', *F.S.* **4**(1), 1982, 10-13; **4**(2), 1983, 31-3. Lee family of Sheffield and Queensland; Featherstone of Crowle, Lincolnshire, 19-20th c.

Leeds, Dukes of
See Osborne

Leetham
LEETHAM, SONYA. 'Great Grandad's round house', *B.T.* **34**, 1998, 7-9. Leetham family, 19-20th c.

Legard
LEGARD, JAMES DIGBY, SIR. *The Legards of Anlaby & Ganton: their neighbours & neighbourhood.* Simpkins, Marshall, Hamilton, Kent & Co., 1926. 16-20th c.; also includes information on other local families, especially Hoby, Dawnay, Cholmley, Hotham, Willoughby, Sykes, Strickland, Constable, Hildyard, Pennyman, Mallory, Creyke, St. Quentin, Grimston, *etc;* also list of vicars of Ganton, 14-20th c.

Legge
PARKIN, TOM. W. 'Robert and Hannah Legge of Beeford, East Yorkshire & Uxbridge, Ontario', *B.T.* **76**, 1998, 27-9. Legge family, 19th c.
SMITH, WILLIAM. 'The family of Dartmouth', *Old Yorkshire* 2nd series **1**, 1889, 164-73. Legge family, Barons Dartmouth, medieval-19th c.

Lelay
See Lethley

Leppington
TOWSE, C.K. 'The Leppington family', *Notes and queries* **221**, 1976, 228-9. 17th c., brief.

Leverthorpe
ROBERTSHAW, WILFRED. 'Two ancient Bradford families', *B.A.* **11**; N.S. **9**, 1976, 29-38. Brief study of the Leverthorpes of Thornton, 14-16th c., and the Appleyards of Allerton, 14-17th c.

Levet(t)
CULLUM, G. MILNER GIBSON. 'Collections relating to the Levett and Hanson families of Melton and Normanton in Yorkshire, *M.G.H.* 3rd series **1**. 1896, 2-9, 51-4, 81-8 & 117-22. Wills, inquisitions post mortem, parish register extracts, and pedigrees, 15-18th c.

SANBORN, VICTOR C. *Thomas Levet of Exeter and Hampton .... with notes on the English and American families of Levett and Leavett.* [ ], 1913. Reprinted from *New England historical and genealogical register* Includes pedigree of Levett of Normanton and Melton, Yorkshire, 15-17th c., subsequently of Exeter and Hampton, New Hampshire.

Levick
CRUMPLER, DIANA. 'The Levick family: from Sheffield 1788 to Australia in 1987: some notes', *F.S.* **9**(1), 1988, 16-18.

Levinge
See Lewen

Lewen
WATSON, T.E., SIR. *History and pedigrees of the family of Lewen of Durham, Northumberland and Scarborough, with pedigrees of their connections, Fulwood, Ker, Rutherford, Radcliffe, and Watson, of Ingleby Greenhow and Newport, Mon., and pedigrees of other families called Lewen, Lewin, Levinge etc., with extracts from wills, public records, etc.* Mitchell, Hughes and Clarke, 1919. Extensive; many pedigrees and extracts from original sources.

SAVAGE, R.A. 'Thank you, Thoresby', *Family tree magazine* **14**(3), 1998, 10. Lewen family of Leeds, 18-19th c.
'A pedigree of the family of Lewen of Amble and Hauxley in the County of Northumberland, and of Scarborough in the county of York', *M.G.H.* 4th series **4**, 1911, 344-54. 17-18th c.

Lewin
See Lewen

Leybourne
LAYBOURN, ROBERT. *The first English admiral, Lord William de Leybourne, and the house of Laybourn from 1025 to 1938.* Copenhagen: privately printed, 1939. Includes branches in Kent, Cumberland and Westmorland, Yorkshire and Denmark.

Leyland
LEYLAND, MARY. 'The Leyland family', *T.Hal.A.S.* 1954, 29-48. 18-20th c.

Lightowler
LIGHTOWLER, J. HALSEY. 'Lightowler', *Bod-Kin* **25**, 1991, 12-13. Lightowler family of Lancashire and Yorkshire, medieval-19th c.

Linton
See Horton

Lister
ARNOLD, H. 'Early Lister emigrants to North America', *T.Hal.A.S.* 1966, 121-4. 18th c.
DENNY, HENRY LYTTELTON LYSTER. *Memorials of an ancient house: a history of the family of Lister or Lyster.* Edinburgh: Ballantyne, Hanson & Co., 1913. Includes pedigrees.
HALLAM, H.A.N. 'The Listers of Frizinghall', *B.A.* **11**; N.S. **9**, 1976, 246-53. 18th c.
RUSHWORTH, PHILIP. 'Lewis Lister', *Bod-kin* **12**, 1988, 4-5. Includes brief pedigree, 19-20th c.
WILSON, J. 'Pedigree of Lister of Shibden Hall', *T.Hal.A.S.* 1956 (Folded pedigree only). 16-19th c.

Lisures
CARTER, W.F., & WILKINSON, R.F. 'Notes on the family of Lisures', *Y.A.J.* **35**, 1941-2, 183-200. Medieval.

Littledale
See Royd(s)

Littlewood
LITTLEWOOD, WILFRED T.D. 'The Littlewood family of Netherthong and Holmfirth, 1510/1988', *Y.F.H.* 14(2), 1988, 36-7.

Lockwood
STEPHENSON, CLIFFORD. 'The Lockwood trail: a look at surname density', *O.W.R.* 5(2), 1985, 32-3. Around Huddersfield.

Lofthouse
L., M.T. 'The Lofthouse family in Cottingham', *Cottingham Local History Society journal* 4(8), 1971, 46-7. 19th c.

Lomas
See Marsden

Longbottom
LONGBOTTOM, ROBIN. 'The Longbottoms: Keighley and district machine makers and mechanics', *O.W.R.* 6(1), 1986, 1-5. 18-19th c.

Longe
See Hassard

Longvillers
CLAY, CHARLES, SIR. 'The family of Longvillers', *Y.A.J.* 42, 1971, 41-51. Includes pedigree, 12-14th c.

Lothrop
MORIARTY, G.ANDREWS. 'Lothrop', *New England historical and genealogical register* 84, 1930, 437-9. Includes extracts from lay subsidies, Star Chamber proceedings, and wills, 16-17th c.

Lovell
'Lovell of Skelton, Yorkshire', *M.G.H.* 2nd series 2, 1888, 259-64. See also 344. Pedigree, medieval-19th c., including Whiteford family.

Lowther
BOUCH, C.M. LOWTHER, & BOUCH, J. LOWTHER. 'Lowther of Ackworth', *Transactions of the Cumberland and Westmorland Antiquarian & Archaeological Society* N.S. 41. 1941, 153-60. 16-18th c., includes pedigree.

BOUCH, C.M. LOWTHER. 'Lowther of Marske (Cleveland) and Holker', *Transactions of the Cumberland & Westmorland Antiquarian & Archaeological Sociey* N.S. 44, 1944, 100-118. Includes folded pedigree, 17-18th c., and monumental inscriptions.

BOUCH, C.M. LOWTHER. 'Lowther of Swillington from its origin till 1788', *Transactions of the Cumberland and Westmorland Antiquarian & Archaeological Society* N.S. 42, 1942, 67-102. Includes folded pedigrees, 17-18th c.

OWEN, HUGH. *The Lowther family: eight hundred years of a family of ancient gentry and worship.* Chichester: Phillimore, 1994. Of Carlisle, Ingleton, and Whitehaven, Cumberland, Marske, Yorkshire, Holker, Lancashire, Swillington, Yorkshire, *etc.* Includes pedigrees, 12-20th c.

Loxley
HUGHES, JOHN. 'The bailliff of Bradfield', *F.S.* 19(2), 1998, 76-82. Loxley family. Medieval-18th c.

HUGHES, JOHN. 'The Loxleys of Hallamshire', *F.S.* 17(4), 1996, 118-22. Includes pedigree, 16-18th c.

Lum
See Mitchell

Lumb
LUMB, G. DENISON. 'Genealogical memoranda relating to the families of Lumb and Wales', *M.G.H.* 3rd series 1, 1896, 132-4. From family bibles, 18th c.

Lumley
LUMLEY, C.C. *Records of the Lumleys, and sketches of the Willey, Williams, and Waters families.* St. Thomas, Ontario: Municipal World, 1908. Of Yorkshire and Canada, medieval-20th c.

Lyster
See Lister

Lyth
'The Lyths, of Newton Pickering', *Y.G.* 1, 1888, 54-7. Includes pedigree, 17-19th c.

Mac Manus
See Sotheron

Maister
INGRAM, M. EDWARD. *The Maisters of Kingston upon Hull 1560-1840.* Todmorden: Waddington & Sons, 1983. Includes folded pedigree.
ROWLEY, JENNIFER C. *The house of Maister.* Hedon local history series **6.** Hedon: Hedon Local History Society, 1982. 18th c.

Malham
See Blackburne

Mallalieu
SYKES, D.F.E. *The Huguenot ancestry of the Mallalieus of Saddleworth.* Marsden: [privately printed], 1920. Includes folded pedigree, 18-20th c.

Mallinson
See Jewett

Mallory
SMITH, S.V. MALLORY. *A history of the Mallory family.* Chichester: Phillimore, 1985. Of various counties, including Yorkshire. 13 pedigrees, medieval-17th c.
See also Legard

Maltby
VERRILL, D. MALTBY. 'Maltby', *Notes & queries* **160,** 1931, 330-32. See also 215 & 394. 14-16th c.
VERRILL, P. MALTBY. 'Maltby of Maltby and Muston', *Notes & queries* **162,** 1932, 437-9; **168,** 1932, 7-9. See also **168,** 1932, 16, 50, 104, 154-5, 210, 268, & 321-2; **169,** 1933, 47-8, 157, 245 & 286. 11-12th c.

Malthouse
WHITELAW, ALBERT J., & GRAY, LES C. *The Malthouse family and their descendants, 1802-1984: a record of the facts available to April 1984 concerning the 9 branches of the families of William Malthouse and Elizabeth Prest who migrated to South Australia from Yorkshire in 1849.* Adelaide: Lutheran Publishing House, 1985.

Mangie
BENNETT, ANN. 'The Mangies of Hull: a family of provincial goldsmiths', *Y.A.J.* **57,** 1985, 149-62. 17-18th c.

Mann
'Extracts from the parish registers of Little Ouseburn, Co., York, of entries relating to the family of Mann, between the years 1565 and 1694', *Genealogist* **7,** 1883, 237-9.

Manningham
ROBERTSHAW, WILFRED. 'Notes on the family of Manningham', *B.A.* **9;** N.S. **7,** 1952, 105-12. Includes folded pedigree, 18th c.

Mansel(l)
See Maunsell

Mantle
REYNOLDS, HY. FITZGERALD. 'Mantle of Hull and Cottingham', *Notes & queries* **152,** 1927, 403-4 & 464-5. 18-19th c.

Marr
THOMPSON, MICHAEL. *The Marr story: the history of a fishing family.* Hull: J. Marr Ltd., 1995. 19-20th c., includes many photographs.

Marsden
PERKINS, ELIZABETH M. *A tree in the valley.* Bognor Regis: New Horizon, 1982. Marsden family, 17-19th c.; also notes on Lawson, Thompson, Lomas, Ogden, Broomhead and Perkins.

Marsh
MURRAY, HUGH. 'Rainwater heads and fall pipe brackets, part V. 69 & 71, Micklegate', *Y.A.S., F.H.P.S.S.N.* **5**(5), 1979, 89-91. Marsh family; includes pedigree, 17-18th c.
POLLARD, SIDNEY. *Three centuries of Sheffield steel: the story of a family business.* Sheffield: Marsh brothers & Co., 1954. Marsh family, 17-20th c.
See also Carr

Marshall
MARSHALL, GEORGE W. 'The Marshalls of Pickering and their descendents', *Y.A.J.* **7,** 1882, 86-111. Includes pedigree, 16-19th c.

RIMMER, W.G. *Marshalls of Leeds, flax-spinners, 1788-1886.* Cambridge: C.U.P., 1960. Includes folded pedigree, 18-20th c.

PLEWS, D. 'Women farmers in the sixteenth century', *Y.A.S. Local History Study Section* 34, 1993, 7-12. Marshall family of Potter Newton.

'Extracts from the parish registers of Egton, near Whitby, co. York', *Genealogist* 2, 1878, 18. Relating to the Marshall family, 1628-1771.

'Extracts from the parish registers of Harswell, co. York', *Genealogist* 2, 1878, 234. Relating to the Marshall family, 18th c.

'Extracts from the parish registers of Holme on Spalding Moor, co. York', *Genealogist* 2, 1878, 233. Relating to the Marshall family, 18th c.

'Extracts from the parish registers of Whitby, co. York, from 1600 to 1795', *Genealogist* 2, 1878, 232-3. Relating to the Marshall family, 17-18th c.

'Extracts from the parish registers of Winteringham, co. York', *Genealogist* 2, 1878, 231-2. Relating to the Marshall family, 16-17th c.

'Marshall', *Genealogist* 1, 1877, 117. 16-17th c. Includes extracts from Middleton parish register.

Martin

EAGARS, KATE. 'The Martins of Cottingham', *B.T.* 17, 1983, 7-8. Includes pedigree, 18-20th c.

TURNER, JOHN M. 'Records in the East Riding Registry of Deeds, Beverley', *B.T.* 11, 1981/2 13-16. Martin family of Sculcoates, 19th c.

Masters

KIDD, L. 'The Masters family', *B.S.H.S.* 15(4), 1985, 66-70. 18-19th c.

Mate

See Walton

Maude

BAILDON, W.PALEY. 'The Maudes of Ilkley, Hollinghall, Brandon, Helthwaite Hill, etc.', in *Miscellanea* [7]. *T.S.* 24, 1919, 137-89. Includes folded pedigree, 16-18th c.

K. 'Maudes of Airedale', *Y.G.* 1, 1888, 71-3. Extracts from parish registers of Bingley, Keighley and Guiseley.

See also Charlesworth

Mauleverer

'Mauleverer pedigree', *M.G.H.* 2, 1876, 73-85. Medieval-19th c.; includes notes from family bible.

Maunsell

STATHAM, EDWARD PHILLIPS. *History of the family of Maunsell (Mansell, Mansel).* 2 vols in 3. Kegan Paul Trench & Co., 1917-20. Of Glamorganshire, Somerset, Carmarthenshire, Northamptonshire, Yorkshire, *etc.*

Mawde

COMBER, JOHN. 'The Mawdes of Riddlesden and Ilkley', *Y.A.J.* 24, 1917, 44-61. Includes folded pedigrees, 16-17th c.

'Mawdes of Burley-in-Wharfedale', *Y.C.M.* 2, 1892, 176. Pedigree, 16-17th c.

'Mawdes of Ilkley', *Y.C.M.* 2, 1892, 175. Pedigree, 16th c.

'Mawdes of West Riddlesden', *Y.C.M.* 2, 1892, 174. Pedigree, 16th c.

Mayall

MEADOWCROFT, MARGARET, & MEADOWCROFT, HARRY. 'The Mayall family of Saddleworth', *B.S.H.S.* 27(4), 1997, 15-21. 17-19th c.; includes pedigrees.

Mayes

See Sayer

Mayson

See Smith

McLean

'The McLean connection with Whitby', *J.Cl.F.H.S.* 3(10), 1988, 25-8. 18-19th c.

Meadowcroft

See Royds

Meaux

CLAY, CHARLES, SIR. 'The family of Meaux', *Y.A.J.* 43, 1971, 99-111. Includes pedigree, 12-14th c.

Mell

PORTEOUS, J. DOUGLAS. 'Place loyalty', *Local historian* **16**(6), 1985 343-5. Proposes methodology for studying continuous occupation of the same place by one family, using the Mell family of Howdenshire, Lincolnshire, and London as an example.

Meller

M[ARSHALL], G.W. 'The Meller family', *Reliquary* **7**, 1866-7, 146. See also 255. Of Almondbury; includes pedigree, 18-19th c.

M[ARSHALL], G.W. 'The Meller family', *Reliquary* **12**, 1871-2, 168-72 & 216. Supplement to previous article; includes pedigree, 18th c., and parish register extracts, 16-18th c.

Mellor

TITTENSOR, E.M. 'Documentary', *O.W.R.* **9**, 1989, 15. Settlement examinations of Samuel Mellor, 1788.

Melvin

HENRY, R.M. 'An Irish family in York', *Y.F.H.S.N.* **16**, 1987, 14-18. Melvin family, 19-20th c.

Metcalfe

GIBSON, DENNY. 'The Metcalfe Society', *Family tree magazine* **8**(7), 1992, 46. Brief note on a one-name society, based in Yorkshire.

METCALFE, WALTER C., & METCALFE, GILBERT. *Records of the family of Metcalfe, formerly of Nappa in Wensleydale.* Mitchell & Hughes, 1891. Not seen.

Meynall

See Sayer

Meynell

AVELING, HUGH, ed. 'The recusancy papers of the Meynell family of North Kilvington, North Riding of Yorks., 1596-1676', in REYNOLDS, E.E., ed. *Miscellanea.* C.R.S. **56**, 1964, 1-112.

HEPPELL, D.A., & HEPPELL, L.T.D. 'The Meynell family at Yarm', *C.T.L.H.S.B.* **13**, 1971, 20-23. 17-18th c.

HEPPELL, D.A., & HEPPELL, L.T.D. 'The Meynell family of Yarm, 1770-1813: a further study', *C.T.L.H.S.B.* **18**, 1972, 11-14.

Middelton

'Middelton of Middelton', *Y.G.* **2**, 1890, 141-4. Medieval-19th c.

Middlebrook

See Stockdill

Middleton

ACRES, WENDY E. 'The story behind the stones', *J.Cl.F.H.S.* **4**(11), 1991, 36-40. Includes pedigree of the Middleton / Morton families, 17-20th c., of Heighington, Northallerton, Hartlepool, *etc.*

Midgley

HARWOOD, H.W. 'Booth Farm and the Midgleys', *T.Hal.A.S.* 1964, 17-29. At Midgley. Midgley family, 14-20th c.

Miller

See Atkinson

Milles

See Salven

Millington

See Watson

Milnes

REDMONDS, GEORGE. 'Surname history: Milnes', *H. & D.F.H.S.J.* **2**(3), 1989, 83.

Mirfin

WATSON, KATHLEEN. 'The Mirfins of South Yorkshire', *F.S.* **16**(4), 1995, 101-5. 16-19th c.

Mitchell

KENDALL, HUGH P. 'High Greenwood in Heptonstall', *P.R.H.A.S.* 1917, 157-80. Mainly concerned with the Mitchell family, 15-18th c.

MITCHELL, J.W. 'Genealogical memoranda relating to the Mitchell family', *M.G.H.* N.S., **3**, 1880, 101-2. Also relating to the Sykes of Yorkshire, 17-18th c.

WOOD, MATTHEW. 'English origins of the Mitchell, Wood, Lum and Halstead families', *Scrivenor* **86**, 1999, 5-10. Of Northowram and New England, *etc.,* 16-17th c.
See also Robertshaw

Molyneaux
See Royd(s)

Monckton
MONKTON, DAVID HENRY. *A genealogical history of the family of Monckton, comprising a full account of Yorkshire and Kentish branches, with some particulars of the principal members of the Nottinghamshire, Staffordshire and Northamptonshire branches.* Mitchell and Hughes, 1887. Extensive; medieval-19th c. Includes many extracts from sources.
'Baron Monckton', *Y.G.* **1**, 1888, 219-24. Monckton family, 19th c.

Moor
See Coles

Morton
'Extracts from the register of Austerfield, Co. York', *M.G.H.* 2nd series **2**, 1888, 331-4. Mainly relating to the Morton and Oldfield families, 16-18th c.
See also Bradfourth, Middleton and Strangwayes

Moser
CHARING, DOUGLAS S. 'The Mosers of Bradford', *O.W.R.* **14**, 1994, 7-8. 19-20th c.

Mosley
SHACKLETON, MICHAEL. 'Pedigree of Mosley', *K.D.F.H.S.J.* Winter 1995, 14-17. 19-20th c.

Mossman
STEVENS, JOAN. 'A note on Mossmans', *Brontë Society transactions* **16**, 1971, 47-50. Of Bradford; includes pedigree showing relationship of Taylor and Mossman, 18-19th c.

Mowbray
MORIARTY, G. ANDREWS. 'Mowbray of Kirklington', *New England historical and genealogical register* **120**, 1966, 170-74. Medieval.
See also Barton

Moxon
REYNOLDS, HENRY FITZGERALD. 'Moxon of Hull, formerly of Pontefract', *Notes & queries* **154**, 128, 453-5. See also **155**, 1928, 88 & 141-2. 15-19th c.; also includes notes on Perrot.

Murgatroyd
C., W.F. 'Murgatroyd of Murgatroyd, *etc.*', *Northern Genealogist* **5**, 1902, 45-6 & 116-8. Includes wills.
MURGATROYD, JOHN BLACKBURN. 'Origin of the name Murgatroyd', *Y.F.H.* **12**(2), 1986, 50-52.
MURGATROYD, J.C. 'Pedigree of Murgatroyd', *K.D.F.H.S.J.* Spring 1986, 14-15. 18-20th c.
See also Ackroyd

Munkton
PEDERSON, FREDERICK. *Romeo and Juliet of Stonegate: a medieval marriage in crisis.* Borthwick paper **87**. 1995. Concerns the marriage of Simon Munkton and Agnes Huntington, mid-14th c.

Murray
See Skeet

Musgrave
MUSGRAVE, PERCY. *Notes on the ancient family of Musgrave of Musgrave, Westmorland, and its various branches in Cumberland, Yorkshire, Northumberland, Somerset etc., compiled mainly from original sources.* Leeds: privately printed, 1911.

Myers
DUSSOME, RENE. 'The Myers family of Yeadon', *Y.F.H.* **17**(3), 1991, 80-83. 19th c.
PALMER, JACK. 'The Myers family, taylors (and musicians)', *F.S.* **12**(1), 1991, 22-5. Of Swinton, 18-20th c.

Nadin
NADIN, DENNIS. 'The Nadin family of Sheffield' *F.S.* 18(3), 1997, 108-9; 18(4), 1997, 131-4. 18-19th c. Also published in *Roots & branches: magazine of the Naden / Nadin Society.*

Nall
GARNER, BARBARA. 'John Nall of Castleton', *F.S.* 7(3), 1987, 65. 18-19th c.

Nalson
LUMB, G.D. 'The Nalson family of Altofts and Methley', in *Miscellanea* [7]. *T.S.* 24, 1919, 368-78. 15-18th c.; includes will of Robert Nalson, 1691.

Neal
'A Neal family bible', *F.S.* 7(2), 1986, 38-9. 19th c., Also includes notes on Johnson family, 19-20th c.

Neave
See Atkinson

Neesam
STEPHENSON, M 'Don't be afraid to ask', *J.Cl.F.H.S.* 4(5), 1990, 36-9. Neesam family, 18-20th c.

Nelson
FOX, MARGARET. 'The Nelsons of Dent', *J.Cl.F.H.S.* 6(12), 1997, 43-4. 18th c.

Nevill(e)
NEVILL, EDMUND R. 'Neville of Thornton Bridge and Cundall', *Genealogist* N.S., 33, 1917, 9-15. Includes pedigree, 13-16th c.
NEVILL, E.R. 'Thorold de Nevill', *Genealogist* N.S., 34, 1918, 117-9. 12-14th c.
WHEATER, W. 'Neville of Liversedge', *Old Yorkshire* 4, 1883, 240-42. 14-16th c.

Newby
'Newby pedigree', *M.G.H.* 2, 1876, 95. 16th c.

Newman
WARD, JOHN NEWMAN, et al. *The Newmans of Barnsley ...* Bath: Ashgrove Press, 1986. Includes pedigree, 18-20th c.

Newnham
See Way

Newsom
BRIGG, J.E. *Memorial of the families of Newsom and Brigg.* Huddersfield: Alfred Jubb and Son, [1898]. Of Wiltshire, London and Yorkshire, *etc,* 16-19th c.
See also Barraclough

Newton
HAZEN, TRACY ELLIOT. 'The ancestry of Ellen Newton, wife of Edward Carlton of Rowley, Mass.', *New England historical and genealogical register* 94, 1940, 1-18. See also 96, 1942, 198-9. 16-17th c., includes extracts from wills, parish registers, lay subsidies, *etc.*
LYDFORD, PAMELA GAYE. 'A Newton saga', *J.Cl.F.H.S.* 6(12), 1997, 39-42. Newton family of Yorkshire and Australia, 19th c.

Nicholls
See Walton

Nicholson
See Colver

Norcliffe
LAWRANCE, HENRY. 'Portraits at Langton Hall in the possession of Francis Best Norcliffe, esq.', *T.E.R.A.S.* 12, 1905, 19-22. Mainly of Norcliffe family members.

Norfolk, Earls of
See Bygod

Norman
See Way

Normanville
SITWELL, GEORGE, SIR. 'Gerard de Normanville', *Genealogist* N.S., 13, 1897, 11-15. Of Yorkshire and Lincolnshire; 12-13th c.

Norris
BRETTON, R. 'The Norrises of Halifax', *T.Hal.A.S.* 1962, 65-93. 18-20th c.

North
REDMONDS, GEORGE. 'Surname history: North', *H. & D.F.H.S.J.* 3(4), 1990, 119.

Northend

NORTHEND, W.F. 'Northend of Little Weighton in the parish of Rowley in the East Riding of the County of York, England, and of Rowley, Massachusetts, U.S.A.', *T.Hunter A.S.* **6**, 1950, 149-63. Includes abstracts of wills and pedigrees, 16-20th c.

NORTHEND, W.F. 'Pedigree of Northend of Northowram in the County of York', *T.Hunter A.S.* **5**, 1943, 91. Folded pedigree 14-20th c.

NORTHEND, W.F. 'The Shibden branch of the Northend family', *T.Hal.A.S.* 1928, 141-51. 16-17th c.

Norton

HUNTLEY, LOCKWOOD. *The Nortons of Norton Conyers and of Rylestone.* Historic Yorkshire Families series. York: North of England Newspaper Co., 1907. Reprinted from the *Yorkshire gazette.* Pamphlet.

See also Sutcliffe

Nussey

'Nussey family tree', *Cameo* 1995, no. 2, 5. 17-19th c.

Nutting

See Colver

Nuvel

DANIELL, CHRISTOPHER. 'Family, land and politics: Ralph Nuvel's family and ancestors in York (c. 1120 - c. 1240)', *York historian* **12**, 1995, 2-20.

Oakes

RODGER, BARBARA. 'Edward Oakes of Attercliffe, scissorsmith', *F.S.* **11**(1), 1990, 24-5. Based on his will, 1689.

Oddie

See Smith

Oddy

GOULD, PETER. 'The elusive Sarah Oddy', *Y.A.S., F.H.P.S.S.N.* **10**(1), 1984, 147-9. Of Baildon, 19th c.

Ogden

DENT, G. 'The Ogden family of clockmakers', *T.Hal.A.S.* 1950, 86-93. 16-18th c.

See also Marsden

Oglethorpe

'Oglethorpe of Oglethorpe' *M.G.H.* 4th series **5**, 1913, 224-5. Pedigree, 15-16th c.

'Oglethorpe of Rawdon', *M.G.H.* 4th series **5**, 1913, 226. 16th c.

Oldfield

REDMONDS, GEORGE. 'Surname history: Oldfield', *H. & D.F.H.S.J.* **4**(4), 1991, 139.

SUTCLIFFE, TOM. 'Stock Lane House, Warley, and the Oldfield family', *P.R.H.A.S.* 1915, 249-78. Includes folded pedigree, 16-19th c.

See also Morton

Oldham

See Leckey

Oldroyd

GOODCHILD, JOHN. 'Mark Oldroyd & Sons of Dewsbury, cloth manufacturers, 1818-1959', *O.W.R.* **4**(1), 1984, 11-13.

See also Ackroyd

Ormesby

See Pulford

Ormondroyd

See Ackroyd

Osborne

LUMB, G.D. 'The Dukedom of Leeds', in *Miscellanea* [5]. *T.S.* **15**, 1909, 1-9. See also 275-6. Osborne family, 17-19th c.

Osgood

See Field

Otes

LISTER, J 'Shibden Hall, Southowram', *P.R.H.A.S.* 1907, 159-90. Includes an account of the Otes family, with pedigree, 15-16th c.

Overend

BELLINGHAM, ROGER A. 'The Overends of New Inn, Pocklington', *B.T.* **37**, 1989, 13-14. 19th c.

Owst

See Smith

Page

See Way

Palmes

TRAPPES-LOMAX, T.B. 'The Palmes family of Naburn, and their contribution to the survival of Roman Catholicism', *Y.A.J.* **40**, 1962, 443-50. See also 665. 16-19th c. 'Palmes of Lindley, Co. York', *M.G.H.* 2nd series **5**, 1894, 40. Includes facsimile of monumental inscription, 1593.

Parker

KEYMER, FAITH. 'The happy marriage', *R.H.* **2**(3), 1993, 50-51. Parker family of Ripon, 19th c.

Description of Browsholme Hall, in the West Riding of the County of York, and of the parish of Waddington, in the same county; also a collection of letters from original manuscripts in the reigns of Charles I and II, and James II, in the possession of Thos. Lister Parker, of Browsholme Hall, esq. S.Gosnal, 1815. Includes folded pedigree of Parker, 16-18th c.
'Parker', *Y.C.M.* **3**, 1893, 111. Brief pedigree, 19th c.

Patchett

PATCHETT, JOHN H. 'Wakefield manor copyholders through six centuries: the Patchetts of Warley, 1350-1900', *T.Hal.A.S.* **5**, 1997, 36-53.

Pawson

BOWMAN, TERRY. 'The Pawson dynasty' *Don. Anc.* **3**(1), 1986, 29-31, **3**(3), 1987, 92-3. Includes pedigree, 19-20th c.

Paxton
See Way

Payne
See Smith and Way

Paynel

ROSS, F. 'The Paynel family', *Old Yorkshire* **2**, 1881, 154-5. Medieval.

Peace

REDMONDS, GEORGE. 'Surname history: Peace', *H. & D.F.H.S.J.* **5**(4), 1992, 139.

Peaker

REDMONDS, GEORGE. 'Surname history: Peaker', *H. & D.F.H.S.J.* **7**(3), 1994, 103. Discussion of the surname.

Pease

FOSTER, JOSEPH. *Pease of Darlington, with notices of the families of Robson, Backhouse, Dixon, and others, being the descendents of Joseph Pease of Shafton in the parish of Felkirk, Yorkshire (1665-1719)*. Privately published, 1891. Includes pedigrees, 18-19th c.
See also Smith

Peck

PECK, S. ALLYN. 'Genealogical research in England: the English ancestry of Joseph Peck of Hingham, Mass., in 1638', *New England historical and genealogical register* **89**, 1935, 327-39; **90**, 1936, 58-67, 194-8, 263-8 & 371-3; **91**, 1937, 7-15, 282-6 & 355-63; **92**, 1938, 71-3; **93**, 1939, 176-8 & 359-61; **94**, 1940, 71-3. See also **92**, 1938, 177-83 & 287-8. Of Suffolk and Wakefield, 15-17th c. Includes wills, Chancery proceedings, *etc.*

Peirse

B[RUCE], W.D. 'Notices of Thimbleby and Ellerbeck, in the parish of Osmotherley, North Riding of Yorkshire, with pedigrees of Peirse, Walton, Hirst and Bayley', *Topographer & genealogist* **1**, 1846, 523-33.

Penny
See Rodes

Pennyman

PATTENDEN, D.W. 'The Pennymans of Ormesby: facts and fallacies', *C.T.L.H.S.B.* **50**, 1986, 12-24. Includes pedigree, 16-18th c.
PEARSON, LYNN F. 'Ormesby Hall, Cleveland', *Y.A.J.* **61**, 1989, 149-54. Home of the Pennyman family, 1600-1961.
MOVERLEY, MARION. 'The Pennymans in Coverdale', *J.Cl.F.H.S.* **5**(5), 1993, 37-40. 17-18th c.
WHYMAN, MARK. 'A close intention to bribery: the Pennyman, Kingsley, Tothill families and the law in the late 16th and early 17th centuries', *C.T.L.H.S.B.* **57**, 1989, 9-16.
See also Legard

Penrose

BALDWIN, A.B. *The Penroses of Fledborough Parsonage: lives, letters and diary.* Hull: A. Brown & Sons, [1933]. 18-19th c., originally of Cornwall.

MC CRACKEN, GEORGE E. 'The Penrose family of Wheldrake and Ballykean, and their descendents in both hemispheres', *New England historical and genealogical register* 116, 1962, 237-55; 117, 1963, 57-70, 106-16 & 195-207. 16-20th c. Ballykean, Co. Wicklow.

PENROSE, CHARLES. *Penrose family of Helston, Cornwall, and Wheldrake, Yorkshire, and Co. Wicklow, Ireland, and other ancestors of James Brinton Penrose* ... Potsdam, N.Y.: Penrose, 1975.

Percy

FONBLANQUE, EDWARD BARRINGTON DE. 'Annals of the house of Percy', *Y.A.J.* 11, 1891, 1-16.

FOWLER, JAMES. 'On two heraldic bench-ends in Great Sandal church', *Y.A.J.* 1, 1880, 132-52. Percy family heraldry, medieval-17th c., includes wills and *inquisition post mortem* for Josseline Percy, 1530.

HUNTLEY, LOCKWOOD. *The Yorkshire Percies.* Hull: A. Brown and Sons, 1954. Includes pedigree, 11-20th c.

STATHAM, S.P.H. 'The parentage of William de Percy', *Y.A.J.* 28, 1926, 101-3. Includes pedigree, 11-12th c.

See also Plumpton

Perkins

See Marsden

Perrott

See Moxon

Peterson

GOODCHILD, JOHN. 'The Petersons: an American mercantile family in Wakefield', *Wakefield Historical Society journal* 3, 1976, 16-21. 18-19th c.

Petty

LEATHER, DAVID. 'The Petty family of Bolton Abbey', *Wh.N.* 8, 1993, 4-6. 17-19th c.

Phillips

PHILIPS, R.B. 'The Phillips family: a Lancashire branch with Yorkshire connections, 1800-1900', *Lancashire: journal of the Lancashire Family History and Heraldry Society* 8(1), 1987, 41-6.

Pickering

PICKERING, JOHN COOPER. 'A lineal descent of the Pickerings of Killington, Crosby Hall, and of Worcester and Yorkshire', *Genealogical quarterly* 3(3), 1934, 285-6.

PICKERING, P. SPENCER UMFREVILLE. *The Pickerings of Barlby, York and Wetherby.* Eyre and Spottiswoode, 1916. 18-19th c.

McKINLAY, R.A. 'The distribution of surnames derived from the names of some Yorkshire towns', in EMMISON, FREDERICK, & STEPHENS, ROY, eds. *Tribute to an antiquary: essays presented to Marc Fitch by some of his friends.* Leopards Head Press, 1976, 165-75. Study of the Pickering surname.

See also Eure

Pickles-Whiteley

BESFORD, JANET. 'Music makers of Finkle Street', *J.Cl.F.H.S.* 5(5), 1993, 34-6. Pickles-Whiteley family of Stockton, 19th c.

Pigot(t)

BRAMHALL, GODFREY. 'Hardwork and serendipity', *R.H.* 2(3), 1993, 59-62. Pigott family; includes pedigrees.

BRAMHALL, GODFREY. 'Pigott of Clotherholme', *R.H.* 1(5), 1991, 4-5. 14-16th c.

FALKINGHAM, CHAS. C. 'Pigot of Melmorby in Coverdale, and of Clotherham, near Ripon, Co. York', *Genealogist* 2, 1878, 294-8.

Pinder

NOCK, D.A. 'The Pinders: an inn keeping tradition', *Journal of the Barnsley F.H.S.* 2(4), 1994, 18-19. Pinder family, 18-19th c.

Plantagenet-Harrison

See Harrison

Platt
KIDD, L.N. 'Some descendents of the Platt family of Thorns, Saddleworth', *B.S.H.S.* **24**(4), 1994, 12-20. 17-19th c.

Plumpton
DOCKRAY, K.R. 'The troubles of the Yorkshire Plumptons in the Wars of the Roses: a West Riding family of Percy retainers whose land-holdings suffered from the Wars of the Roses and from legal disputes', *History today* **27**, 1977, 459-66 & 482. 15-16th c.
KIRBY, JOAN W. 'A fifteenth-century family: the Plumptons of Plumpton and their lawyers, 1461-1515', *N.H.* **25**, 1989, 106-19.
KIRBY, JOAN W. 'A northern knightly family in the waning middle ages', *N.H.* **31**, 1995, 86-107. Plumpton family of Plumpton Hall.

Pollard
See Burton

Pontifex
See Bullen

Pope
HUNTER, JOSEPH. *Pope: his descent and family connexions: facts and conjectures.* John Russell Smith, 1857. 17-18th c., includes notes on the Turner family.
See also Turner

Porter
See Colver

Portyngton
HUNT, JOHN G. 'The early Portyngtons of Portington', *New England historical and genealogical register* **116**, 1962, 166-76. 13-15th c.

Postlethwaite
See Craven

Potter
BORN, SHARON. 'The Potter family in the Tadcaster area', *C.Y.D.F.H.S.J.* **35**, 1995, 21. 18-19th c.
MEINERTZHAGEN, GEORGINA. *From ploughshare to Parliament: a short memoir of the Potters of Tadcaster.* Rev. ed. John Murray, 1908. 18-19th c.

Power
'Original certificate of a marriage by a Justice of the Peace', *Y.A.J.* **34**, 1939, 8. Marriage of William Power of Halifax and Mary Wormall, 1653.
'Pedigree of the Power family', *P.R.H.A.S.* 1917, 30-31. 16-17th c.

Poynton
See Blackburne

Prickett
PRICKETT, F. FENTON. *The Pricketts of Allerthorpe.* Mitchell, Hughes and Clarke, 1929. Includes folded pedigrees, 17-20th c., wills, Chancery proceedings, *etc.*

Prest
See Malthouse

Priestley
PRIESTLEY, PAUL. *A history of the surname Priestley.* [ ], [199-?] Centred on Bradford.
See also Roberson

Priestman
PRIESTMAN, S.H. *The Priestmans of Thornton Le Dale and some of their descendants: their religious labours and creaturely activities intermixed with extracts from the earliest records of the monthly meetings of the people call'd Quakers*, ed. Stephen Doncaster & James Dent Priestman. 2nd ed. York: The editors, in association with William Sessions, 1986. 16-19th c., includes pedigrees.
See also Richardson

Procter
'Procter', *K.D.F.H.S.J.* Summer 1999, 14-15. Pedigree, 19-20th c., of Colne.
See also Richardson

Pulford
SITWELL, GEORGE, SIR. *The barons of Pulford in the eleventh and twelfth centuries and their descendents, the Revesbys of Thrybergh and Ashover, the Ormesbys of South Ormesby, and the Pulfords of Pulford Castle, being a historical account of the lost baronies of Pulford and Dodleston in Cheshire, of seven knights' fees in Lincolnshire attached to them, and of many manors, townships and families in both counties.* Scarborough: Sir George Sitwell, 1889. Includes deed abstracts, medieval.

Pulleyn

PULLEIN, CATHARINE. *The Pulleyns of Yorkshire.* Leeds: J.W. Whitehead & Son, 1915. Extensive, medieval-20th c. Includes pedigrees, extracts from Knaresborough court rolls, Duchy of Lancaster ministers' accounts, subsidy and hearth tax rolls, extracts from registers of numerous parishes and marriage licenses, lists of wills, feet of fines, *etc., etc.*

Radcliffe

'Pedigree of the family of Radcliffe of Milnes Bridge and Rudding Park, Co. York', *M.G.H.* 4th series **3**, 1910, 2-5. 18-19th c.

'Shaw Hall, Saddleworth, and the Radcliffe family', *Palatine note-book* **3**, 1883, 210-12. Medieval.

See also Lewen and Slinger

Radman

RADMAN, PETER. 'Radman, Ridman and Rudman in North Yorkshire, West Yorkshire, and Lancashire: variants of Redman', *Lancashire: [journal of the Lancashire Family History and Heraldry Society]* **11**(2), 1990, 35-40.

Raikes

FOSTER, JOSEPH. *Pedigree of Raikes, formerly of Kingston upon Hull.* Phillimore & Co., 1930. 16-20th c., also of Bennington, Gloucestershire, Treberfydd, Breconshire, Llwnegrin, Flintshire *etc.*

Raimes

RAIMES, ALWYN LESLIE. *The family of Raimes of Wheldrake.* [ ]: privately published, 1966. 11-20th c., includes pedigrees.

Raine

CHOICE, LEOPOLD. 'Raine', *Pedigree register* **1**, 1907-10, 224-5. Of Richmond, London, *etc.;* pedigree, 18-19th c.

Ramsden

HARGREAVES, J.A 'The Halifax Ramsdens', *Wesley Historical Society (Yorkshire Branch) [newsletter]* **49**, 1986, 5-9. 19th c.

RAMSDEN, J.W. 'The Ramsdens of Hull', *B.T.* **54**, 1993, 30-31. 19th c.

Ransome

See Atkinson

Raper

WRIGHT, H.R. 'Over a century of farming by the Raper family in Cottingham', *Cottingham Local History Society journal* **11**(2), 1990, 39-43. 19-20th c.

Rasby

'Pedigree of Rasby', *Genealogist* **1**, 1877, 92-6. See also **2**, 1878, 30 & 96-9; **4**, 1880, 108. 13-17th c.

Raughton

PETCH, M.R. 'The Raughton family influence on the curvilinear style', *Y.A.J.* **58**, 1986, 37-55. 14th c.

Rawdon

ARMITAGE, H. 'The Rawdon family', *T.Hal.A.S.* 1967, 37-53. 17-19th c.

DAVIES, ROBERT, ed. *The life of Marmaduke Rawdon the second of that name.* Camden Society **85**. 1863. Includes pedigree, 16-18th c.

Rawlins

RAWLINS, COSMO W. H. *Family quartette: the families of Rawlins of Stoke Courcy (Somerset), Hooper of Devonport and Maidstone, Smith-Wyndham of E. Yorks, and Russell (Dukes of Bedford).* Yeovil: the author, 1962.

Rawson

PORRITT, ARTHUR. 'The Rawson family', *T.Hal.A.S.* 1966, 27-52. 18-20th c.

See also Royd(s)

Rayner

KENDALL, H.P., & TRIGG, W.B. 'The Rayners of Norland', *T.Hal.A.S.* 1931, 113-32. Medieval-17th c.

RAYNER, DAVID K. 'Village blacksmiths: the Rayners of Burley', *B.A.* 3rd series **4**, 1989, 18-24. Includes pedigree, 18-19th c.

Reaney

ROGER, M. 'Reaney of Greenhill', *F.S.* **2**(3), 1980, 62-4. 16-18th c.

Redma(y)n(e)

DUCKETT, GEORGE, SIR 'Harwood evidences: Redman of Harwood and Levens', *Y.A.J.* 4, 1877, 84-95. Includes pedigree, medieval.

GREENWOOD, W. 'The Redmans of Harewood Castle, Yorkshire', *Northern genealogist* 5, 1902, 54-68. 14-16th c., includes *inquisitions post mortem,* wills, *etc.*

GREENWOOD, WILLIAM. *The Redmans of Levens and Harewood: a contribution to the history of the Levens family of Redman and Redmayne in many of its branches.* Kendal: Titus Wilson, 1905. Medieval-17th c.; includes pedigree of Redman of Ireby, 15-17th c, and many others.

GREENWOOD, W. 'The Redmaynes of Levens', *Northern genealogist* 5, 1902, 212. Medieval.

GREENWOOD, W. 'A sketch of the history of the Redmaynes of Levens, Harewood, and Thornton in Lonsdale', *Northern genealogist* 4, 1902, 105-12. Medieval.

PARKER, JOHN. 'The Redmans of Yorkshire', *Y.A.J.* 21, 1910-11, 52-90. Medieval.

REDMAN, J.C. 'The Redman family of Jerrys Plain, N.S.W.', *J.Cl.F.H.S.* 3(12), 1988, 32-5. 18-19th c., originally of North Yorkshire.

'Family of Redman or Redmayne of Harewood, Co. Ebor.', *M.G.H.* N.S., 3, 1880, 441-2. Pedigree, 13-16th c.

Remington

PRETTYMAN, WILLIAM. 'The Remingtons of Craven, Yorkshire', *Genealogist* N.S., 27, 1911, 129-49.

Reresby

'A crossbar licence, 1516', *Genealogist* N.S., 10, 1894, 248-9. For Reresby of Yorkshire.

Restwold

See De La Vache

Revesby

See Pulford

Reynoldson

See Henderson

Rhodes

BANKS, F. '[Yorkshire born Rhodes family members in Manchester, from censuses, 1851-71]' *Y.A.S., F.H.P.S.S.N.* 11, 1976, 154-5. List.

HOYLE, FRETWELL W. 'Rhodes pedigree', *M.G.H.* 2, 1876, 158-9. 18-19th c.

NOCK, DEBORAH A. 'The Rho(a)des family: a genealogists dream', *J. Barnsley F.H.S.* 5(1), 1997, 15-17. 19th c.

NOCK, D.A. 'The Rho(a)des family: a genealogists dream', *Y.F.H.* 19(4), 1993, 86-7. 18-19th c.

PADGETT, L. 'Great Houghton Hall and the Rhodes family', *Y.N.Q.II* 3, 1907 4-5. 17-19th c.

REDMONDS, GEORGE. 'Surname history: Rhodes', *H. & D.F.H.S.J.* 8(3), 1995, 107. 'Rhodes of Lotherton, parish [of] Sherburn in Elmet', *Northern genealogist* 2, 1896, 176. Parish register extracts and monumental inscriptions, 17-18th c.

Rich

HEY, DAVID. 'The Riches of Bullhouse: a family of Yorkshire dissenters', *N.H.* 31, 1995, 178-93. Rich family of Bullhouse, Penistone.

Richardson

BOYCE, ANNE OGDEN. *Records of a Quaker family: the Richardsons of Cleveland, with portraits of Isabel Casson, Jonathan Priestman, and John Richardson Procter, also nine genealogical tables, and an index to the marriages.* Samuel Harris & Co., 1889. 17-19th c.

DALE, THOMAS CYRIL. *The descendants of Robert Richardson (who died A.D. 1705) of Great Woodhouse in the township of Leeds, Co. York.* Solicitors Law Stationary Society, 1924. 18-19th c.

LEIGHTON, H.R. 'Bible entries, *etc.:* family of Richardson of Robin Hood's Bay, Bishopwearmouth, and Sunderland', *M.G.H.* 4th series 1, 1906, 322-3. 18-19th c.

RICHARDSON, GEORGE. *The annals of the Cleveland Richardsons and their descendants compiled from family manuscripts, etc.* Newcastle upon Tyne: [ ], 1850. 18-19th c.

SHEERAN, GEORGE. 'The Richardsons and their garden at Brierley Hall', *B.A.* 3rd series **4**, 1989, 3-10. 17-18th c.
'Richardson of Lassell Hall, Kirkheaton', *Y.G.* **2**, 1890, 106-8. 17-19th c.
'Richardson pedigree', *Y.C.M.* **1**, 1891, 354. Of Bradford, 17th c.
'Some account of the probable ancestry of the Rev. Christopher Richardson, M.A., Trin. Coll., Camb., of Lascelles Hall and rector of Kirkheaton, Yorkshire', *Northern genealogist* **2**, 1896, 9-12. Includes folded pedigree, 16-19th c.
See also Smith

Richmond
CHIPPINDALL, W.H. 'On the family of de Richmond, constables of Richmond Castle, and their connection with Corby', *Transactions of the Cumberland and Westmorland Antiquarian and Archaeological Society* **16**, 1916, 97-9. Medieval.
RICHMOND, KEITH C. 'The Richmond Surname Society', *J.Cl.F.H.S.* **1**(2), 1980, 38-9.

Rickard
REYNOLDS, FITZGERALD. 'Rickard of Tickhill, near Doncaster, afterwards of Kingston-upon-Hull', *Notes and queries* **152**, 1927, 455-8.

Ridehalgh
See Aspinall

Ridman
See Radman

Rigge
'[Rigge pedigree]', **3**, 1893, 121. 17th c. Of Halifax.

Riley
REDMONDS, GEORGE. 'Surname history: Riley', *H. & D.F.H.S.J.* **7**(2), 1994, 67. Discussion of the surname.
See also Robertshaw

Rimmington
RIMMINGTON, WILLIAM HENRY. 'The family of Rimmington, of Gateforth in the parish of Brayton, near Selby, in the County of York (West Riding)', *Genealogist* N.S., **36**, 1920, 92-105.

Roberson
NUSSEY, JOHN T.M. 'Hammond Roberson of Liversedge (1754-1841): bully, or gentleman? *Y.A.J.* **53**, 1981, 97-109. Includes pedigree of Ashworth and Priestley, showing his wife's descent.

Roberts
ROBERTS, SAMUEL, et al. *Some memorials of the family of Roberts of Queen's Tower, Sheffield and Cockley Clay, Swaffham, Norfolk, as exemplified by kindred, affinity and marriage.* 4th ed. Sheffield: J.W. Northend, 1862. Includes folded pedigree, 17-20th c.
STEELE, IRMA. 'The Roberts family of West Yorkshire and South Australia', *Y.F.H.* **19**(1), 1993, 22-3. 18-19th c.
'Northern counties pedigrees', *M.G.H.* 5th series **10**, 1938, 18-19, 43-7, 82-5 & 100-1. Pedigrees of Roberts, Winter, Wadsworth and Hussey, all of Sheffield; also Smith of Ecclesfield and Crawthorne of Crawthorne.

Robertshaw
ROBERTSHAW, R. 'My grandfathers' grave', *F.S.* **18**(4), 1997, 127-9. Robertshaw family, 18-20th c.
ROBERTSHAW, WILFRED. 'Annals of a West Riding family', *B.A.* **11**, N.S. **9**, 1876, 275-93. Robertshaw family, 16-20th c.
'Robertshaw, Riley and Mitchell families', *M.G.H.* 2nd series **4**, 1892, 168. Of Todmorden; extracts from family bible, 17-18th c.

Robertson
BULLOCH, M. 'Dame Madge Kendall's Robertson ancestors', *Notes and queries* **163**, 1932, 398-400, 418-20 & 434-7. Of York and Lincolnshire, 18th c.

Robinson
GAWTHROP, HUMPHREY. 'The friendly Robinsons', *K.D.F.H.S.J.* Winter 1996, 16-18. 19th c.
GAWTHROP, H. 'Pedigree of Robinson', *K.D.F.H.S.J.* Spring 1999, 14-15. 18-19th c.
HALL, DAVID. *Richard Robinson of Countersett and the Quakers of Wensleydale.* York: William Sessions, 1989. Not seen. Includes pedigree.

HINCHLIFFE, G. 'The Robinsons of Newby Park and Newby Hall', *Y.A.J.* **63**, 1991, 127-38; **64**, 1992, 185-202; **65**, 1993, 143-52. 16-19th c.

PERKINS, JOHN P. 'Elith Robinson and the I.G.I.', *J.Cl.F.H.S.* 5(6), 1992, 41-3. Of Northallerton, Husthwaite, *etc.,* 19th c.

ROBINSON, JOHN. 'The connection of a Kendal family with Rokeby', *Cumberland and Westmorland Antiquarian and Archaeological Society transactions* N.S. **6**, 1906, 171-2. Robinson family, 18-19th c. 'Family found - and lost', *Y.A.S., F.H.P.S.S.N.* 8(4), 1982, 59-60. Pedigree of Robinson of Leeds, *etc.,* 18-19th c.

Robson

CLAGUE, CHERYL. 'The Robsons of Yorkshire and Durham', *Y.F.H.* 18(2), 1992, 37-8. 17-19th c.
See also Cutsforth and Smith

Rodes

BOUMPHREY, R.S. 'The Rodes family of Horbury, Co. York', *Y.A.J.* **41**, 1966, 117-28. Includes pedigrees of Rodes, 16-18th c.; also of 'Wright, Staveley, Colton-Fox, Penny and Boumphrey, showing the descent from Rodes of Horbury'.

Roebuck

REDMONDS, GEORGE. 'Surname history: Roebuck', *H. & D.F.H.S.J.* 3(1), 1989, 25.

ROEBUCK, ARTHUR W. *The Roebuck story.* Toronto: A.W. Roebuck, 1963. Of Sheffield and Canada, *etc.,* 16-20th c.

Rokeby

BARTLETT, R. GROSVENOR. 'Rokeby family: Bible fly leaves', *Northern genealogist* **3**, 1900, 37-8. 17th c.

ROKEBY, RALPH. *Oeconomia Rokebiorum: an account of the family of Rokeby.* ed. A.W. Cornelius Hallen. Supplement to *Northern notes & queries, or, the Scottish antiquary* **1**. Edinburgh: David Douglas, 1887.

Rookes

ROBERTSHAW, WILFRED. 'A local conversation piece', *B.A.* **8**; N.S. **6**, 1940, 398-402. Discussion of a portrait of the Rookes family, 18th c.

TURNER, J. HORSFALL. 'Early notices of the Rookes family', *B.A.* **1**, 1888, 20-25. Includes pedigree, 15-17th c.
See also Atkinson

Roos
See Ingilby

Roundell
'The Roundells of Gledstone', *Old Yorkshire* **5**, 1884, 191-3. 16-19th c.

Routh
'Slight sketch of the history of the ancient family of Routh', *Y.G.* **1**, 1888, 233-8. Medieval.

Rowlerson

ROWLERSON, MICHAEL A. 'Rowlersons in York, 1894-1982', *C.Y.D.F.H.S.N.* **38**, 1996, 20-22.

Rowntree

ROWNTREE, C. BRIGHTWEN. *The Rowntrees of Riseborough.* [2nd ed.] York: William Sessions, 1982. Also of Easby. Includes pedigrees, 17-19th c.

Royd(s)

HANSON, T.W. 'Royds of George Street, Halifax and of Bucklersbury, London', *T.Hal.A.S.* 1941, 75-83.

R. 'The Royds of Rishworth', *P.R.H.A.S.* 1904-5, 283-8. 15-18th c.

ROYDS, CLEMENT MOLYNEUX, SIR. *The pedigree of the family of Royds.* Mitchell Hughes and Clarke, 1910. 18-19th c., includes pedigrees of Beswicke, Calverley, Clegg, Gilbert, Hudson, Littledale, Meadowcroft, Molyneaux, Rawson, Smith and Twemlow.
See also Akroyd

Ruddy

RIDDY, JUDY. *Yorkshire innkeepers: a most accomodating family,* ed. Alison Goulty and Nichola Roberts. Whitley Bay: Judy Ruddy, [1995?] Ruddy family, 19-20th c.

Rudman
See Radman

Rudston
'Hayton notes', *T.E.R.A.S.* 11, 1903, 123-5.
Extracts from Hayton parish register
relating to the Rudston family, 17-18th c.;
includes folded pedigree.

Ruggles
See Way

Rushforth
See Collingwood

Rushworth
RUSHWORTH, PHILIP. 'Chartism and Philip
Rushworth', *Bod-Kin* 19, 1990, 9-10.
Includes pedigree, 19-20th c.

Russell
See Rawlins

Rutherfurd
See Lewen

Rutter
See Le Roter

Ryther
BROWN, W. 'A Yorkshire knight in the
fifteenth century', *Reliquary* N.S., 5, 1891,
112-3. Ryther family.

Sagar
SAGAR, JOHN H. 'Sager / Sager (early variants
Saiger / Sayger / Sagger / Segar / Seagar /
Seager / Sieger)', *F.S.* 7(3), 1987, 68-9. Of
Lancashire and the West Riding;
discussion of a one-name study.
SAGAR, JOHN H. 'Sagar / Sager (and early
Saiger / Sayger / Sagger / Segar / Seagar /
Seager / Sieger variants)', *Y.F.H.* 13(3), 68-
9. Brief discussion of an extensive one-
name study.
'Sagar / Sager, and early Saiger / Sayger /
Sagger / Segar / Seagar / Seager / Seiger
variants', *Y.F.H.S.N.* 14, 1986, 28-9. One
name study; of Lancashire and Yorkshire.

Saint Paul
HORNE, J. FLETCHER. 'Concerning the
surname and arms of the family of
Saint Paul', *Y.A.J.* 20, 1908-9, 284-90.
Medieval.

St. Quentin
See Legard

St. Quinton
ELLIS, A.S. 'Notes on some ancient East
Riding families and their arms V. The De
St. Quintons', *T.E.R.A.S.* 10, 1903, 19-24.
Medieval.

Salkeld
MOORE, J. GRAINGE. *Salkelds through seven
centuries.* Phillimore, 1988. Of
Cumberland, Yorkshire, Suffolk,
Shropshire and Cheshire; includes
pedigrees, probate records, *etc.*

Saltmarshe
SALTMARSHE, PHILIP. *History of the
township and family of Saltmarshe in the
East Riding of Yorkshire.* York: Ben
Johnson and Company for private
circulation, 1910. Including pedigrees, 12-
19th c.

Saltonstall
FOLEY, PETER. 'The illustrious Saltonstalls',
Family tree magazine, 6(9), 1990, 13-14. Of
Yorkshire and Essex, includes pedigree,
14-17th c.
JONES, K.R. 'The Saltonstall family from
Pontefract', *Notes & queries* 215, 1970,
165-8. 17-18th c.

Salven
GIBBONS, ALFRED. 'Salven v. Milles: an old
matrimonial dispute', *Northern
genealogist* 6, 1903, 74-8. Depositions,
1534.

Salvin
KENDALL, HUGH P. 'Newbiggin in Egton and
the Salvin family', *Y.A.J.* 33, 1938, 87-104.
Medieval-18th c.
See also Hoole and Whitaker

Sandwith
S[ANDWITH], L.. *The Sandwiths of Helmsley,
Co., York: a short preliminary pedigree.*
Phillimore & Co., 1897. 16-19th c.
SANDWITH, L. *The Sandwiths of the City of
York.* Tanganyika: Vuga Mission, 1921.
16-17th c.

Saunderson
See Hoole

Savil(l)e
BAILDON, W. PALEY. 'Notes on the early Saville pedigree and the Butlers of Skelbrook and Kirk Sandal', *Y.A.J.* **28**, 1926, 380-419; **29**, 1929, 68-89. Medieval, includes pedigree.

CLAY, J.W. 'The Saville family', *Y.A.J.* **25**, 1908-9, 1-47. 13-17th c., includes wills.

BRETTON, ROWLAND. 'The Savile family', *T.Hal.A.S.* 1968, 55. Medieval-17th c.

LISTER, J. 'Bradley Hall: the home of a distinguished family', *P.R.H.A.S.* 1919, 1-28. Saville family, 16-17th c.

NUTTALL, BARBARA H. *The Saviles of Thornhill: life at Thornhill Hall in the reign of Charles I.* Leeds: B.H. Nuttall, 1986.

ROSS, FREDK. 'The family of Savile', *Old Yorkshire* 2nd series **2**, 1890, 149-73. Medieval-19th c.

SAVILLE, ALAN. 'Tales of mystery or imagination', *F.S.* 3(3), 1982, 65-7. Saville family of Sheffield, 18-19th c.

Saxton
FORDHAM, GEORGE, SIR. 'Christopher Saxton of Dunningley: his life and work', in *Miscellanea* [9]. *T.S.* **28**, 1928, 357-84. See also 491. Includes pedigree, 17th c., and a survey of Burley, 1602.

R[OBERTSHAW], W. 'A Saxton family note', *B.A.* **9**; N.S. **7**, 1952, 217-8. 16-17th c.

Sayer
SAYER, J.P. 'The Sayer family of Worsall', *E.C.A. [English catholic ancestor] journal* 2(5), 1988, 107-13; 2(6), 1988, 137-42. 16th c.

WARDELL, JOHN W. 'The recusants of the Friarage, Yarm, Yorkshire', *Recusant history* **8**, 1965-6, 158-65. Sayer, Maynes and Meynall families, 17-19th c.

Scambler
BIRD, ALAN. 'Scambler', *Y.A.S., F.H.P.S.S.N.* 5(3), 1979, 62-4. Scambler family, 18-19th c.

Scarr
SCARR, J.R. 'Extracts from *A history of the Scarr family*', *Y.A.S., F.H.P.S.S.N.* 9(1), 1983, 25-6; 9(3), 1983, 38-40; 9(4), 1983, 98-9.

Scarth
'The surname of Scarth', *Cameo* 1996, no. 2, 3-6. Medieval-19th c.

Scatcherd
'Scatcherd of Bishop Monkton', *Northern genealogist* **1**, 1895, 142. Pedigree, 17-18th c.

Scholey
ALLEN, DEREK. 'An Alladin's cave', *F.S.* 3(4), 1982, 93-4. Scholey family, 18-19th c.

Scott
BODDINGTON, REGINALD STEWART. 'Pedigree of Scott', *M.G.H.* 3rd series **1**, 1896, 204-8. Of York, 17-19th c.

MATERI, MAUREEN. 'The Scott family', *K.D.F.H.S.J.* Winter 1997, 25. Brief notes on a Keighley family, 19-20th c.

WELLSTED, BILL. 'Links with York', *Y.F.H.* 15(6), 1989, 131-2. Notes on the Scott family, 19th c.

Scottowe
THORNTON, C.E. 'The Scottowe family of Ayton', *C.T.L.H.S.B.* **35**, 1978, 12-15. 18th c., including pedigree.

Scriven
See Boyle

Scrope
ELLIS, A.S. 'Notes on some ancient East Riding families and their arms', *T.E.R.A.S.* **11**, 1903, 19-30. Notes on Scrope of Flotmanby, De Carethorpe of Carethorpe, and Thorpe of Thorpe juxta Howden; medieval.

HUNTLEY, LOCKWOOD. *The Scropes of Bolton Castle and of Masham.* York: the Yorkshire Gazette, 1904. Pamphlet, medieval.

METCALFE, JOHN HENRY. *A great historic peerage: the Earldom of Wiltes.* Chiswick Press, 1899. Scrope family of Danby on Yore, 14-19th c.

RAINE, J. 'The Scropes, in connection with York Minster', *Associated Architectural Societies reports and papers* 6(1), 1861, 46-51. 15th c.

Seagar
See Sagar

Sedgwick

HUGHES, BARBARA. 'The Sedgwick family of Sedbergh and Dent', *K.D.F.H.S.J.* Spring 1997, 10-11. Includes pedigree, 16-19th c.

O'BRIEN, CHRISTOPHER. 'John Sedgwick of Ripon and his family', *R.H.* 3(2), 1996, 50-53; 3(3), 1996, 68-9 & 72-4. Includes pedigree, 17-18th c.

PINDER, JANE. 'The Sedgwick family', *Wh.N.* **26**, 1997, 20-21; **27**, 1998, 19-20. 18-19th c.

ROBINSON, GILLIAN. 'The Sedgwicks: shepherds and gamekeepers in the South Yorkshire Pennines', *O.W.R.* **12**, 1992, 26-30. 19th c.

Segar

See Sagar

Sedman

SEDMAN, GARRIOCH. *Sedman or Caedmon? A personal journey through the history of the Sedman family of Hackness, Fylingdales and Barrowfield, 1500-1945.* Broadstone, Dorset: G. Sedman, 1995. Medieval-19th c., includes pedigrees.

SEDMAN, G. 'The Sedman Hospital of Scarborough', *B.T.* **74**, 1998, 26-30; **75**, 1998, 28-30. Mainly concerns the Sedman family, 17-18th c., includes probate inventory of Thomas Sedman, 1714.

Seebohm

CUDWORTH, WILLIAM. 'The Seebohm family of Bradford, Yorks., and Hitchin, Herts.', *B.A.* N.S. **1**, 1900, 113-21. 19th c.

Seiger

See Sagar

Serjeantson

SERJEANTSON, R.M. *The Serjeantsons of Hanlith.* 2 pts. [Northampton: Mark, 1908]. Pt. 2 only seen. 14-19th c., includes folded pedigree.

Sessions

See Atkinson

Shackleton

BUTTERWORTH, P.C. 'Pedigree of Shackleton', *K.D.F.H.S.J.* Summer 1996, 14-15. 18-20th c.

ROGAN, N. 'Pedigree of Shackleton', *K.D.F.H.S.J.* Autumn 1996, 14-15 & 17. 19-20th c.

'Pedigree of Shackleton', *K.D.F.H.S.J.* Spring 1995, 12-13. 17-20th c.

Shaftoe

SHAFTO, ROBERT. *The Shaftoes of York.* Walkerscraft Publishing, 1992. Medieval-20th c., includes wills of William Shafton, 1476, and Richard Shafton, 1705.

Shafton

See Shaftoe

Shawe(e)

BROOKES, STANLEY. 'The Shaws of South Yorkshire in the seventeenth century', *F.S.* 11(2), 1990, 39-40.

GREENWOOD, DENNIS. *James Shaw, Son & Co., bellfounders & clockmakers of Bradford, Yorkshire.* Meltham: Dennis Greenwood, 1996. Shaw family; includes pedigree, 19-20th c.

PEDGLEY, DAVID. 'The Shaw family of Boarshurst', *B.S.H.S.* 25(3), 1995, 5-12; 25(4), 1995, 8-13. Includes pedigree, 17-18th c.

SHAW, R.M. 'The Shaws of Stainland', *T.Hal.A.S.* 1965, 45-69. 18-20th c.

KING, M.F. 'Shawe', *New England historical and genealogical register* **49**, 1895, 64. Extracts from Halifax registers, 1590s.

Sheffield

See Way

Shepherd

BROOKE, SHIRLEY. 'The Shepherds of Appleton-le-Moors', *Ryedale historian* **19**, 1998-9, 4-6. Shepherd family, 19th c.

SHEPHERD, PETER, & BLAIR, ROBERT. *Genealogical tables of the family of Robert and Ann Shepherd.* Adelaide: Flair Publishers, 1993. Of Yorkshire and Australia, 19-20th c.

SHEPHERD, PETER. *Simple annals: the emigration of Robert and Ann Shepherd to South Australia, 1843.* Adelaide: Shepherd Family Reunion Committee, 1993. 18-20th c.

Shepley
LUMB, G.D. 'Shepley pedigree', *Northern genealogist* **2**, 1896, 199-205. Includes folded pedigree, 18-19th c., Wills, monumental inscriptions, extracts from a family bible and from newspapers, *etc.* *See also* Carew

Sherburn
'Thomas Sherburn of Adwick le Street', *Don. Anc.* **5**(2), 1991, 238-44. 18-19th c.

Sherwood
SHERWOOD, MARY 'Back in time with the Sherwoods', *Y.F.H.S.N.* **16**, 1987, 6-8. 17-20th c.

Shiers / Shires
ANDREW, D.M.G. 'Pedigree of Shires (or Shiers)', *K.D.F.H.S.J.* Winter 1997, 14-15. 18-20th c.

Shore
STEPHEN, LADY. 'The Shores of Sheffield and the Offleys of Norton Hall', *T.Hunter A.S.* **5**, 1943, 1-17. 17-19th c.

Short
See Hassard

Shrimpton
SHEPHERD, BILL. 'The Shrimpton highwayman', *J.Cl.F.H.S.* **1**(2), 1980, 31-7. 17-18th c.

Sidgwick
See Benson

Simms
See Craven

Simpson
SIMPSON, STEPHEN. *Simpson: records of the ancient yeoman family of the West Riding of Yorkshire, 1544-1922.* Bemrose and Sons, 1922. Includes pedigree, 16-20th c., deed abstracts, *etc.*
SIMPSON, STEPHEN. 'Simpson', *Pedigree register* **1**, 1907-10, 64-7 & 340-43. Of Preston, Lancashire and Gisborne, Yorkshire, pedigrees, 16-20th c.
See also Baxter

Sinclair
See Atkinson

Siswick
REDMONDS, GEORGE. 'Surname history: Siswick', *H. & D.F.H.S.J.* **5**(2), 1992, 67.

Skaife
BICKLEY, SUSAN. 'In search of the Skaife D'Ingerthorpes', *R.H.* **3**(10), 1988, 264-6. Skaife family, medieval-19th c.

Skeet
History of the families of Skeet, Somerscales, Widdrington, Wilby, Murray, Blake, Grimshaw and others. Mitchell Hughes and Clarke, 1909. Skeet of Surrey, Somerscales of Grimsby and Hull, Widdrington of Northumberland, Wilby of Northamptonshire, Murray of Felton Hall, Shropshire, Blake of Ireland, Grimshaw of Lancashire; includes pedigree.

Skilleto
SHILLETO, ROWLAND JAMES. 'The Skilletos of the West Riding of Yorkshire', in *Miscellanea* **[8]**. *T.S.* **26**, 1924, 282-310. Medieval-19th c.

Skottowe
SKOTTOWE, PHILIP F. *The leaf and the tree: the story of an English family.* Research Publishing, 1963. Skottowe family of Norfolk, Yorkshire, Buckinghamshire, *etc.* Medieval-20th c.
WALL, MARIAN. 'The Skottowes of Norwich and Great Ayton', *J.Cl.F.H.S.* **4**(12), 1991, 49-50. 17-18th c.

Slinger
POSTLETHWAITE, REG. 'More surprises from North Yorkshire', *Y.F.H.* **17**(3), 1991, 75-6. Slinger, Tempest and Radcliffe families; includes pedigree, 16-17th c.

Slingsby
HUNTLEY, LOCKWOOD. *The Slingsbys of Scriven and of Red House.* Historic Yorkshire families series **9**. York: North of England Newspaper Co., 1905. Reprinted from the *Yorkshire gazette*. Pamphlet.

PITTS, SUSAN E.E. 'The Slingsbys of Scriven, c.1600-1688: rivalry, status and local government', *N.H.* **33**, 1997, 88-107.

Smeaton
See Hall

Smellie
See Leckey

Smith
BRYANT, EDITH. 'Smith of Thornecombe, Devon, Smith of Cawood, nr. Selby Yorkshire', *Devon and Cornwall notes and queries* **16**, 1930-31, 296-8.

NICHOLLS, GORDON A. 'J. Smith family of Thurgoland, contemporaries of Walton emigrants to Auckland', *F.S.* **12**(4), 1992, 97-9. 19th c.

HANSOM, J.S. 'Family notes of Thomas Owst's descendents, the Smiths of Drax', in *Miscellanea* 1. C.R.S. 1. 1905, 137-42. 18th c.

SMITH, DAVID T. 'The Smiths of Yorkshire and Glen Sherr: an agricultural family', *T.Hunter A.S.* **8**(2), 1960, 77-98; **8**(3), 1961, 157-61. 16-20th c.

SMITH, DOUG. 'Marriages in the Smith family of Great Givendale and Givendale Grange', *R.H.* **3**(12), 1998, 315. List, 18-19th c.

SMITH, GEO. H. 'The Smiths of Halifax', *T.Hal.A.S.* 1949, 73-91. Includes folded pedigree, 17-19th c.

SMITH, HENRY ECROYD. *Annals of Smith of Cantley, Balby and Doncaster, County York, embracing elaborate pedigrees of the connected families and biographical notices of their more eminent members.* [Sunderland: Hills & Co.], 1878. Not seen. Includes pedigrees of Kilholm or Killam, Aldam, Stacye or Stacie, Payne, Stepney, Gulston or Gulson, Akroyd or Ecroyd, Oddie, Robson, Hedley, Pease, Dixon, Coates, Richardson, Mayson, Dearman, Waterhouse, Barton, Clough, Hagen, Tyson, Whalley, Harrison and Darby.
See also Benson, Owst, Roberts and Royd(s)

Smith-Wyndham
See Rawlins

Smithies
SMITHIES, JOHN. 'A long line of Lancelots', *Y.F.H.* **21**(5), 1995, 113-5. Smithies family; includes pedigree, 16-20th c.

Smythe
See Way

Snowdon
HARRINGTON, J. 'The Snowdons: a study of a Cleveland family', *J.Cl.F.H.S.* **2**(12), 1985, 20-24.

Somerford
See Atkinson

Somerscales
See Skeet

Sonley
TURNER, JOHN M. 'An East Riding surgeon and apothecary', *B.T.* **49**, 1992, 17-19. Sonley family; includes pedigree, 18-19th c.

TURNER, JOHN M. 'Tracing back to George Sonley, officer in the Excise', *C.Y.D.F.H.S.J.* **28**, 1992, 22-4; **33**, 1994, 12-14. Sonley family, 18-19th c.

TURNER, JOHN M. 'Where did the Sonleys come from?' *B.T.* **28**, 1986, 11-13. 18-19th c.

Sorby
SORBY, WM. HERBERT. *Genealogy of the Sorby family.* Waterlow & Sons, 1895. Includes folded pedigrees, 16-19th c.

Sotherne / Sotheron
SOTHERAN, CHARLES. 'Sotherne and Sotheron families', *M.G.H.* N.S., **1**, 1874, 217-23. Of London and Yorkshire; includes pedigrees, 17-19th c., and grants of arms.

SOTHERAN, CHARLES. *Genealogical memoranda relating to the family of Sotheron, of counties Durham, Northumberland, York, etc., and to the sept of Mac Manus.* Taylor and Co., 1871. 15-19th c., includes pedigrees.
See also Watson

Southcott
THOMPSON, CHRISTINE. 'The foundling who survived', *Family tree magazine* **13**(1), 1996. 57-8. Southcott family, 18-19th c., includes discussion of Foundling Hospital (Thomas Coram Foundation) records.

Speke

MURDOCH, SOPHIA. *Record of the Speke family (Jordans, Somerset)*. Reading: H.T. Morley, [1900]. Of Somerset, Devon, Yorkshire, Lancashire, Wiltshire and Berkshire.

Spencer

STIRLING, A.M.W. *Annals of a Yorkshire house, from the papers of a Macaroni & his kindred.* 2 vols. John Law, 1911. Spencer and Stanhope families, 17-19th c.

WOLEDGE, HENRY. 'Rekindling the sparks of Spencer', *Y.A.S., F.H.P.S.S.N.* 7(4), 1981, 143-4. Spencer family, 19-20th c.

'The Spencers of Cantley', *Don. Anc.* 6(2), 1993, 47-9. Includes abridged pedigree, 18-19th c.

'Spencer of Bramley Grange', *R. & D.F.H.S.N.* 2, 1984, unpaginated (3pp). 17-19th c.

See also Hall

Spivey

REDMONDS, GEORGE. 'Surname history: Spivey', *H. & D.F.H.S.J.* 1(4), 1988, 91.

Spooner

TADMAN, MARGARET. 'Spooner in the Washburn Valley', *Wh.N.* 16, 1995, 24-6. 18-19th c., of Norwich and Fewston.

Squire

'Squire genealogy', *Family history* 2(10), 1964, 110-23. Of Doncaster; pedigree, 16-19th c.

Stacie / Stacye

See Smith

Stainrod

See Ackroyd

Stancliffe

REDMONDS, GEORGE. 'Surname history: Stancliffe', *H. & D.F.H.S.J.* 8(4), 1995, 143.

Stanhope

GILDERSOME-DICKINSON, G.E. 'Dugdale's visitation of Yorkshire, with additions: Stanhope of Hampull', *Genealogist* N.S., 13, 1897, 208.

See also Spencer

Staniforth

H[EXT], F.M. *Stanforthiana, or the family of Stanforth of Darnall in Yorkshire.* Bristol: Lavars, 1863. Medieval-19th c., includes pedigrees.

Stanley

See Atkinson and Way

Stansfeld

STANSFIELD, JOHN. *History of the family of Stansfeld of Stansfield in the parish of Halifax and its numerous branches.* Leeds: Goodall and Suddick, 1885. Extensive; includes pedigrees, medieval-19th c., and many extracts from original sources.

Stapelton

CHETWYND-STAPYLTON, H.E. *The Stapeltons of Yorkshire, being the history of an English family from very early times.* Longmans Green and Co., 1897. Revision of papers originally printed in the *Y.A.J.* Includes pedigrees, medieval-19th c.

CHETWYND-STAPYLTON, H.E. 'The Stapeltons of Yorkshire', *Y.A.J.* 8, 1884, 65-116, 223-58, 381-423 & 427-74. Includes folded pedigrees, medieval-19th c.

CHETWYND-STAPYLTON, H.E. [Letter concerning the Stapelton family]', *Y.A.J.* 13, 1895, 315-8. See also 481-5.

Staveley

See Rodes

Stedman

See Barton

Stephenson

BROWN, ROMA K. 'Family history: Richard Stephenson, medical practitioner, 1831/2-1867', *J.Cl.F.H.S.* 2(1), 1982, 15-18. Of Pickering and Australia.

CARPENTER, JOAN E. 'The Stephensons of Arras', *B.T.* 47, 1991, 15-18. Includes pedigree, medieval-20th c.

See also Appleyard

Stepney

See Smith

Sterne

CLAY, J.W. 'The Sterne family', *Y.A.J.* **21**, 1910-11, 91-106. Includes pedigree, 17-18th c., and wills.

Stickney

NICHOLAS, ELAINE C. 'Elizabeth, wife of William Stickney of Rowley, Massachusetts', *New England historical and genealogical register* **139**, 1985, 319-21. Notes on the Stickney, Dawson and Burrell families of Cottingham, 16-17th c.

Stockdill

STOCKDILL, ROY. 'The Stockdill / Middlebrook connection', *Cameo* 1998, no. 2, 6-11. Includes pedigree, 18-20th c.

STOCKDILL, ROY. 'The Stockdills', *C.Y.D.F.H.S.J.* **41**, 1997, 7-8. 18-19th c., with note on a one name society.

Stocks

WARRINGTON, D. 'The Stocks family of Upper Shibden Hall', *T.Hal.A.S.* 1971, 67-86. 19-20th c.

Storey

See Coates

Storm

STORM, ALAN. *Storm and company.* Whitby: Caedmon, 1993. Not seen. Storm family of Robin Hoods Bay.

Storr

BOULTER, W. CONSITT. 'The book of remarks of William Storr, of Scalm Park, 1678-1731', *Y.A.J.* **7**, 1882, 44-62. Includes folded pedigree of Storr of Hulton-Bushell and Scalm, notes on births and burials, extracts from a rental of Wistow, 1711 *etc.*

WILSON-BARKWORTH, A.B. *Notes on the families of Storr of Hilston and Owstwick, in Holderness in the East Riding of Yorkshire.* Cambridge: Macmillan and Bowes, 1890. Includes folded pedigree, 17-19th c.

Strangwayes

MORTON, EDWARD. 'Strangwayes', *M.G.H.* N.S., **1**, 1874, 20-21. Extracts from Sneaton parish register, 17-18th c.

'Strangwayes and Morton pedigree', *M.G.H.* N.S., **3**, 1880, 23-4. Folded pedigree, 17-19th c.

Strickland

See Legard

Strother

NOCK, DEBORAH A. 'In search of the Strothers', *F.S.* **13**(3), 1993, 69-71. 18-19th c.

Stubbs

STUBBS, WILLIAM. *Genealogical history of the late Bishop William Stubbs,* compiled by himself, ed. Francis Collins. *Y.A.S., R.S.* **55**. 1915. Extensive pedigrees of Stubbs and related families, 14-19th c., also many extracts from original sources.

Stukeley

LUKIS, W.C., ed. *The family memoirs of the Rev. William Stukeley, M.D., and the antiquarian and other correspondence of William Stukeley, Roger and Samuel Gale, etc.* Surtees Society **73**, **76** & **80**. 1882-7.

Styan

KENDALL, DAVID. 'Styan of Whixley', *R.H.* **2**(5), 1994, 96-100. Medieval-19th c.

Styring

STYRING, HAROLD K. *Earls without coronets (the Styr dynasty).* Sheffield: Hartley & Son, 1965. Styring family, medieval-18th c., of Sheffield, the United States, *etc.*

STYRING, H.K. *The royal heirs of Canute in South Yorkshire.* Sheffield: the author, 1961. Pamphlet; Styring family.

Sugden

HOLMES, HAZEL. 'The Sugdens of Eastwood House', *K.D.F.H.S.J.* Winter 1993, 6-7. 18-20th c.

Sunderland

'Capt. Langdale Sunderland', *Y.G.* **1**, 1888, 208-13. Sunderland family, 16-19th c.

'High Sunderland', *P.R.H.A.S.* 1907, 113-38. Includes much information on the Sunderland family, 13-17th c.

Sutcliffe
WILSON, JOHN. 'Sutcliffes of Ovenden', *T.Hal.A.S.* 1955, 47-60. 18-19th c., includes the will of Frances Norton, 1765.

Swaine
See also Eure

Swainson
HEALY, HOPE FRANCIS. *An historical narrative of a Swainson family from the West Yorkshire and Lancashire counties of England.* Deborah, Iowa: Anundsen Publishing, 1993. Includes pedigree, 16-20th c.

Swift
See Colver

Swillington
BEANLANDS, [ARTHUR]. 'The Swillingtons of Swillington', in *Miscellanea* [5]. *T.S.* 15, 1909, 185-211. Medieval-16th c.

Swire
SWIRE, J. 'Pedigree of the Swire family of Craven', *K.D.F.H.S.J.* Spring 1994, 14-15. 17-20th c., subsequently of London.
SWIRE, JACK. 'Information for Swire researchers', *K.D.F.H.S.J.* Spring 1995, 20-21. Of Yorkshire, Lancashire, *etc.;* census extracts, 1851.

Sydenham
See Danby

Sykes
BLAKEBOROUGH, JOHN F.F. *Sykes of Sledmere: the record of a sporting family and famous stud.* Philip Allan & Co., 1929. 17-20th c.
PAMELY, MONICA. 'A billhead bonanza', *H. & D.F.H.S.J.* 7(4), 1994, 112-3; 8(1), 1994, 8-9. Sykes family of Golcar, 19th c.
'Extracts from parish registers', *M.G.H.* N.S., **3**, 1880, 102-4. Sykes family, 18-19th c.
See also Eure, Legard and Mitchell

Sylvester
HUNTER, JOSEPH. *Gens Sylvestrina: memorials of some of my good and religious ancestors, or, eleven generations of a puritan family.* J.B. Nichols & Son, 1846. Sylvester family, 16-19th c.

Talbot
BOWLER, HUGH. 'Venerable John Talbot: some genealogical notes', *Recusant history* **4**, 1957-8, 217-22. 16th c. North Riding family.
'Talbot and Braddyll memoranda', *M.G.H.* N.S., **3**, 1880, 200. Probably of Yorkshire, 16-17th c.

Tankard
MEGSON, JOHN R. 'Bolling Hall and the Tankards', *Bod-Kin* **29**, 1992, 16-18. 19th c.

Tatham
'Pedigree of Tatham of Yorkshire', *K.D.F.H.S.J.* Autumn 1994, 14-15. 18-19th c.

Taylor
WOOLRICH, GILL. 'Unrepeated connections: the Taylor trail', *C.Y.D.F.H.S.N.* **20**, 1989, 3-4. Of Yorkshire and Shropshire, *etc.,* 19-20th c.
POLLARD, SIDNEY, & TAYLOR, ROBERT. 'Profit-sharing and autocracy: the case of J.T. and J. Taylor of Batley, woollen manufacturers, 1892-1966', *Business history* **18**, 1976, 4-34.
See also Mossman and Way

Telford
HARVEY, JOHN H. 'The family of Telford, nurserymen of York', *Y.A.J.* **42**, 1971, 352-7. Includes folded pedigree, 18-19th c.

Tempest
LANCASTER, M.E. *The Tempests of Broughton.* Broughton Hall: H.R. Tempest, 1987. 11-20th c.
TEMPEST, E.B., MRS. 'The Tempest family of Bowling Hall', *B.A.* N.S. **1**, 1900, 491-511. 16-17th c.
See also Slinger

Tenison
TENISON, C.M. 'Tenison', *M.G.H.* 3rd series **2**, 1898, 141-8. Of Yorkshire and Norfolk; pedigrees, 16-19th c.
TENISON, C.M. 'Tenisonia', *M.G.H.* 4th series **3**, 1910, 204-10. 16-17th c.

Thackray
THACKRAY, CATHERINE. 'Thackray research', *Y.F.H.* 21(2), 1995, 31-2; 21(5), 1995, 119-20; 21(6), 1995, 141-2. 17-19th c.

THACKRAY, CATHERINE. ' 'Father and son', *Y.A.S., F.H.P.S.S.N.* 6(2), 1980, 15-17; 6(3), 1980, 31-3. Thackray family, 19th c.

Thanet, Earls of
See Tufton

Thewlis
REDMONDS, GEORGE. 'Surname history: Thewlis', *H. & D.F.H.S.J.* 2(4), 1998, 107.

Thirlway
DENTON, JEAN, ed. 'The Thirlway journal', *R.H.* 2(1), 1993, 2-6. Includes Thirlway pedigree, 18-19th c.

Thistlethwaite
THISTLETHWAITE, B. *The Thistlethwaite family: a study in genealogy.* Headley Brothers, 1910. 17-19th c., includes many pedigrees.

Thom
THOM, WILLIAM A. 'The Rev. William Thom (1751-1811) and some of his descendants', *Wesley Historical Society (Yorkshire Branch) [newsletter]* 72, 1998, 14-18.

Thomas
PORTER, ANN. 'The Thomases of Haworth', *K.D.F.H.S.J.* Summer 1998, 16-19. 18-20th c.
THACKRAY, CATHERINE. 'A Thornhill family: cultivators of gardens and children', *O.W.R.* 11, 1991, 27-31. Thomas family, 19th c.

Thompson
BANKS, MARJORIE. 'Benjamin Blaydes Thompson', *B.T.* 76, 1998, 35. Thompson family, 18th c.
REYNOLDS, HY. FITZGERALD. 'Merchant adventurers: Thompson of Newcastle upon Tyne (afterwards of Kingston-upon-Hull)', *Notes & queries* 152, 1927, 274-7. See also 320-1, 376, 428 & 444-5. 15-19th c.
ROBINSON, ARTHUR R.B. *The counting house: Thomas Thompson of Hull (1754-1828) and his family.* York: William Sessions, 1992.
Sheriff Hutton Park and the Thompson family. Occasional papers 2. York: York Georgian Society, 1946. Contents:
EGERTON, J. 'Sheriff Hutton Park'.
PRESSLY, I.P. 'The Thompsons of Sheriff Hutton Park'. 18th c.
See also Marsden

Thoresby
ALEXANDER, G. GLOVER. 'An old case for the opinion of counsel relating to the property of the Thoresby and Briggs families', in *Miscellanea* [9]. *T.S.* 28, 1928, 405-16.
ELLIS, A.S. 'Notes on Ralph Thoresby's pedigree', in *Miscellanea* [3]. *T.S.* 9, 1899, 112-25. Medieval-17th c.

Thornhill
CLAY, C.T. 'The family of Thornhill', *Y.A.J.* 29, 1929, 286-321. Medieval; includes folded pedigree.

Thornton
THORNTON, ALICE. *The autobiography of Mrs. Alice Thornton, of East Newton, Co. York,* [ed. Charles Jackson]. Surtees Society 62. 1875. Includes folded pedigrees of Thornton, 14-19th c., and Wandesford, 16-17th c.

Thorpe
HUNT, JOHN G. 'Early history of the family of Thorpe next Welwyk', *New England historical and genealogical register* 114, 1960, 217-27. Medieval.
WILLIAMS, VINA. 'The Thorpe family of Gleadless', *F.S.* 9(2), 1988, 50-52. Extracts from family Bible, 18-20th c.
See also Scrope

Threapland
CARPENTER, STELLA H. 'A Wibsey medical family', *B.A.* 3rd series 4, 1989, 53-9. Threapland and Warburton families, 18-19th c.

Thwaite
THWAITE, H.T. 'A Yorkshire family: the Thwaites of Marston, West Riding of Yorkshire, 1323-1641', *Genealogists magazine* 10(15), 1946, 9-13.

Thwaytes
'Descent of Frances, daughter of Sir Henry Thwaytes, kt., and wife of John Gresham', *M.G.H.* N.S., 4, 1884, 117. Medieval.

Tillotson
CLARKE, JOAN M. 'The Tillotson family of Calderdale and Luddenden Foot (1730?-1910)', *Scrivenor* 84, 1998, 14-15. 18-19th c.

Tindall

TINDALL, CHRISTIAN. *The Tindalls of Scarborough, descendants of Ralph Tyndale, of North Grimston.* Exeter: William Pollard & Co., 1927. 15-20th c., includes pedigrees.

Tinker

REDMONDS, GEORGE. 'Surname history: Tinker', *H. & D.F.H.S.J.* 4(3), 1991, 107.

Tordoff

KEYWORTH, RUTH. 'The name of Tordoff', *Bod-Kin* 42,1996, 20-23. Medieval-19th c.

Tothill

See Pennyman

Town

TOWN, ALAN. 'The Town family history', *Y.F.H.* 19(1), 1993, 5-7; 19(2), 1993, 29-31; 19(3), 1993, 58-9. Of Lincolnshire and Yorkshire, 19-20th c.

Tranmer

TRANMER, KENNETH. 'On the trail of Tranmers', *B.T.* 24, 1985, 6-7. Tranmer family, 19-20th c.

Trattles

See Cole

Travis

'The Travis family', *Cottingham Local History Society journal* 4(34), 1975, 222-6. 17-19th c.

Trenholme

TRENHOLME, EDWARD CRAIG. *Trenholme in Yorkshire, with some notes on the Trenholme family.* Oxford: A.T. Broome & Son, 1938. Medieval-19th c.

Tufnell

TUFNELL, E.B., et al. *The family of Tufnell, being some account of the Elizabethan Richard Tuffnayle and his descendants, with a chapter on the properties of Langleys, Nun Monkton, and the manor of Barnsbury.* Privately printed, 1924. Of Essex, Yorkshire and Middlesex.

Tuke

SESSIONS, WILLIAM K., & SESSIONS, E. MARGARET. *The Tukes of York in the seventeenth, eighteenth and nineteenth centuries.* York: Sessions Book Trust, Ebor Press, 1971.

Tufton

Memorials of the family of Tufton, Earls of Thanet, deduced from various sources of authentic information. Gravesend: Robinsons, 1800. Of Kent, Yorkshire, *etc.*, medieval-18th c.

Tupholme

'Tupholme and Banks', *F.S.* 1(1), 1977, 13-17. 17-19th c.

Turner

B[RUCE], W.D. 'Turner famly of Kirkleatham, North Riding of Yorkshire', *Topographer & genealogist* 1, 1846, 505-9.

NORTHCLIFFE, CHARLES BEST. 'Pope's maternal ancestry', *Genealogist* 4, 1880, 150-53. Turner family of York, 16-17th c.

DAVIES, ROBERT. *Pope: additional facts concerning his maternal ancestors.* John Russell Smith, 1858. Turner family of York, 16-17th c.

RODGER, MARGERY. 'Why was he named Francis Drake?', *F.S.* 6(2), 1985, 43-6. Turner and Drake families, 16-19th c.

TURNER, ALAN. 'The Turners of South Yorkshire', *Don. Anc.* 3(1), 1986, 10-11. Lists parish registers in which the surname has been found.

See also Fawkes and Pope

Twemlow

See Royd(s)

Tyack

TYACK, F.G. 'Operation ancestors', *F.S.* 1(3), 1978, 56-7. Includes Tyack family pedigree, 19-20th c.

Tyerman

RAHAMUT, ANNE. 'A due for ever', *J.Cl.F.H.S.* 5(10), 1994, 28-30. Tyerman family of Northallerton, early 19th c.

Tyndale
See Tindall

Tyson
See Smith

Tyzack
TYZACK, DON. *Glass tools and Tyzacks.* 2nd ed. Gerrards Cross: Don Tyzack, 1995. Of Kingswinford, Newcastle upon Tyne, Sheffield, Stourbridge, *etc.,* 16-20th c.

Ullathorne
KENTISH, BASIL LEONARD. *The chronicles of an ancient Yorkshire family: the Ullathornes, or Ullithornes of Sleningford and some of their descendants, 1450-1960.* Kelvedon: the author, 1963. Includes separate folded pedigree, 16-19th c.

Umfreville
[PICKERING, EDWARD ROWLAND.] *The Umfrevilles: their ancestors and descendants.* Clapham: Battens, [1855?] Medieval-19th c., also includes pedigree of Pickering.

Umpleby
See Coates

Underhill
See Field

Upton
See Way

Urwick
URWICK, THOMAS A. *Records of the family of Urswyck, Urswick or Urwick,* ed. William Urwick. St. Albans: Gibbs & Bamforth, 1893. Of Lancashire, Yorkshire, Shropshire, London *etc.,* medieval-19th c. Includes folded pedigrees, 17-19th c.

Uttley
UTTLEY, D. 'Origin of the family name of Uttley (or Utley)', *Y.F.H.* 12(6), 1986, 135-6.

Vantier
See Wanty

Vasey
BAINES, DOROTHY. 'Too many reverends', *Y.F.H.* 21(6), 1995, 138-40. Vasey family, 18-19th c.

Vavasour
'A pedigree of the family of Vavasour, of Spaldington, in Yorkshire', *M.G.H.* 1, 1868, 193-6. 12-18th c.
See also Brocas

Ventress
PORTER, ANDREW. 'Ventress family', *Cameo* 1994, no. 3, 17-18. Of Gildersome, *etc.,* includes pedigree, 19-20th c.

Ver
MASSINGBERD, W.O. 'Ver of Battesford and Goxhill, Co. Lincoln, and Sproatley, Co. York', *Genealogist* N.S., **20**, 1904, 73-7. 12th c.

Vernatti
'Vernatti family', *Fenland notes & queries* **6**, 1904-6, 30-2 & 55-9. See also 85-8 & 133-9; **7**, 1907-9, 135. 17-18th c.

Vescy
BOWLES, C.E.B. 'Vescy of Brampton-en-le-Morthen, in the parish of Treeton, Co. York, and their descendants', *Y.A.J.* **17**, 1902-3, 340-70. Includes wills, deeds, monumental inscriptions, *etc.* Vescy family, medieval-17th c., Bradshaw family, 17th c., Galliard family, 18-19th c.

Vickerman
CHAPMAN, KEN, & CHAPMAN, EILEEN. 'The Vickerman family of Holderness', *B.T.* **13**, 1982, 19-21. 18-20th c.

Vincent
BODDINGTON, REGINALD STEWART. 'Pedigree of the family of Vincent', *M.G.H.* 4th series **3**, 1910, 89-91. 15-18th c.

Waddington
'The Rev. Dr. Waddington', *Y.C.M.* **4**, 1894, 9-11. Includes pedigrees, 18-19th c.
See also Bullen

Waddy
WADDY, J. LEONARD. *The Waddy family.* Bognor Regis: W.M.H.S. Publications, 1982. Medieval-20th c.

Wade
'Pedigree of Wade', *K.D.F.H.S.J.* Winter 1994, 14-15. 19-20th c.

Wadsworth
See Roberts

Wagstaff
KENT, BARBARA. 'The Wagstaffs of Foxhouse, Holmfirth', *Y.F.H.* 21(4), 1995, 93-4. 18-19th c.

Wainman
'The Wainman family', *Y.N.Q.II.* 2, 1906, 19. 18-19th c.

Wakefield
See Whitaker

Walker
BRETTON, ROWLAND. 'Walkers of Crow Nest', *T.Hal.A.S.* 1971, 101-22. At Lightcliffe; 17-19th c.
HEY, DAVID G. 'The nailmaking background of the Walkers and the Booths', *T.Hunter A.S.* 10(1), 1971, 31-6. 18th c.
'Famous local families, I: the family background of Samuel and Aaron Walker', *F.S.* 1(1), 1977, 17-20. Includes will of Joseph Walker of Stubbin House, Ecclesfield, 1729.
'Walker of Halifax', *Y.C.M.* 3, 1893, 64-70. 18-19th c.
See also Collingwood and Hall

Walton
MILNER, R.H. 'Some family statistics', *O.W.R.* 2(1), 1982, 35-6. Walton family, 18th c.
NICHOLLS, G.A. 'Yorkshire Walton-Mate background and associations with Thurgoland wire mills', *F.S.* 18(3), 1997, 100-102; 18(4), 1997, 136-41; 19(1), 1998, 30-34. 17-19th c.
NICHOLLS, GORDON A. 'Mainly about Walton and Nicholls strays from around Sheffield and district', *F.S.* 12(2), 1991, 41-5. 19th c.
See also Peirse and Smith

Walwyn
See Bullen

Wandesford(e)
M'CALL, HARDY BERTRAM, ed. *Story of the family of Wandesforde, of Kirklington & Castlecomer, compiled from original sources, with a calendar of historical manuscripts.* Simpkin Marshall Hamilton Kent & Co., 1904. Castlecomer is in Co. Kilkenny. The appendix calendars 269 deeds, mainly relating to Yorkshire.
'The Wandesfordes of Kirklington', *Ancestor* 10, 1904, 98-103. 14-17th c.
See also Thornton

Wanty
PEET, HENRY. *Genealogical memoranda relating to the Huguenot family of de Vantier, Anglais Wanty.* Privately printed, 1902. Includes folded pedigree; of Lincolnshire, Cambridgeshire and Yorkshire.

Warburton
See Threapland

Warenne
LOYD, L.C. 'The origin of the family of Warenne', *Y.A.J.* 31, 1934, 97-113. Medieval.

Waring
See Atkinson

Washington
NEWSOME, W. *Yorkshire as the home of the Washingtons.* Newcastle on Tyne: privately published, [1879]. Includes 36 Washington pedigrees.

Waterhouse
LISTER, JOHN. 'Shibden Hall: the Waterhouse family', *P.R.H.A.S.* 1910, 109-32; 1913, 159a-60; 1915, 149-52; 1916, 261-92; 1917, 53-88. 16-17th c.
PORRITT, A. 'Well Head and the Waterhouses', *T.Hal. A.S.* 1958, 63-76. Waterhouse family, 13-19th c.
See also Smith

Waters
See Lumley

Waterton

HALL, H. ARMSTRONG. 'Some notes on the personal and family history of Robert Waterton of Methley and Waterton', in *Miscellanea* [5]. *T.S.* **15**, 1909, 81-102. 15th c.
See also Burgh

Watkins
See Wilmer

Watmore / Watmough

WHATMORE, GEOFFREY. *Watmough people: roots of a North Country family.* Pershore: G.Whatmore, 1998. Not seen
WHATMORE, GEOFFREY. *Wat's brother-in-law: episodes and origins of the Watmough, Watmore and Whatmore families.* 9 fiche. Kent Family History Society record publications **51**. 1985. Of Lancashire, Yorkshire, Canterbury, London, *etc.,* includes pedigrees.

Watson

SHEPPARD, WALTER LEE. 'The Watson ancestry of Constance (Brigham) Crosby of Holme-upon-Spalding Moor, Yorkshire, and Rowley, Mass., and notes on the Sotheron and Millington families', *New England historical and genealogical register* **120**, 1966, 21-5. See also 231. 16th c.
WATSON, T.E. 'A pedigree of the family of Watson of Ingleby-Greenhow in the County of York', *M.G.H.* 5th series **2**, 1916-17, 13-21. 16-20th c.
See also Lewen

Wawne

WAWN, CHARLES NEWBY. *Wawn family records.* 5 pts. Sunderland: Hills Press, 1926. Medieval-18th c., many wills.

Way

WAY, HERBERT W.L. *History of the Way family: a record in chronological order of members of the Way family of Bridport, Co. Dorset, Denham Place, Co. Bucks., Spencer Grange and Spaynes Hall, Co. Essex, from the earliest records to the present time, with full or partial pedigrees of Page of Wricklemarsh,*
Newnham of Maresfield, Hills of Poundsford, Payne, Lord Sheffield, Lord Stanley of Alderley, Cooke, Taylor of Ogwell, Ruggles, Brise of Spains Hall, Smyth of Ashton Court, Kenrick of Woore, Ffarington of Worden, Cotrell Dormer of Rousham, Upton of Ingmire, Paxton of Durham, Norman of Claverham, etc. Harrison & Sons, 1914.

Weatherhead

STREET, A.E. 'Weatherhead or Wetherill?' *R.H.* **3**(7), 1997, 176-7. 19th c.

Weatherill

WEATHERILL, JAMES BLACKWOOD. 'The Weatherill family', *C.Y.D.F.H.S.J.* **41**, 1997, 22-3. 19th c.

Webb

'Copied from a family bible dated 1633', *B.T.* **17**, 1983, 5. Webb family, 18-19th c.

Webster

WEBSTER, JOHN. 'The whaling Websters', *B.T.* **43**, 1990, 15-16. 19th c.

Weddell

OAKES, EDWARD. 'Is your name Weddell?' *Y.F.H.* **15**(2), 1989, 49-50. Pedigree, 18-20th c.

Wedg(e)wood

WEDGEWOOD, LES, & WEDGEWOOD, MARGARET. 'The Wedg(e)woods of Yorkshire', *Y.F.H.* **19**(2), 1993, 46-7. Of Coxwold and Whitby, 17th c.
WEDGEWOOD, LESLIE. 'Wedgewood: a recusant branch in North-East Yorkshire', *Catholic ancestor* **4**(2), 1992, 51-7. Includes pedigree, 18-19th c.
WEDGEWOOD, MARGARET. 'The Esk Valley Wedg(e)woods', *J.Cl.F.H.S.J* **7**(2), 1998, 38-40. 18-19th c.

Weightman
See Wightman

Wentworth

CHESTER, JOSEPH LEMUEL. 'A genealogical memoir of the Wentworth family of England from its Saxon origins in the eleventh century to the emigration of one of its representatives to New England about the year 1636', *New England historical and genealogical register* **22**, 1868, 120-39.

MILNER, R.M. 'Wentworth Woodhouse and its owners', *Y.A.J.* **6**, 1882, 343-84. Wentworth family.
WENTWORTH, GEORGE EDWARD. 'History of the Wentworths of Woolley', *Y.A.J.* **12**, 1893, 1-35 & 159-94. Medieval-19th c.

West

'The West family of Mortomley', *F.S.* 3(3), 1982, 63. List of births, 1788-1832.

Westby

SOTHERAN, CHARLES. 'Westby pedigree', *M.G.H.* N.S., **1**, 1874, 445-8. 13-19th c.
'Westby pedigree', *M.G.H.* **2**, 1876, 217. Medieval-16th c.

Wetherill

See Weatherhead

Whalley

See Smith

Wharncliffe

See Wortley

Wharton

ROSS, F. 'The Wharton family', *Old Yorkshire* **2**, 1881, 156-60. 17-18th c.

Whatmore

See Watmore / Watmough

Wheelwright

LONGBOTHAM, A.T. 'Clay House, Greetland under the Wheelwright ownership', *T.Hal.A.S.* 1934, 115-45. 17-18th c.

Wheler

WHELER, GEORGE HASTINGS. ed. *Hastings Wheler family letters, 1693-1704.* Wakefield: Chiswick Press, 1929. Letters of Lady Betty Hastings of Ledstone.
WHELER, GEORGE HASTINGS, ed. *Hastings Wheler family letters, 1704-1739.* Wakefield: West Yorkshire Printing Co., 1935. Letters of Lady Betty Hastings of Ledstone.

Whitaker

WEBB, PATRICIA. 'A drop of Yorkshire blood?' *Y.F.H.* **17**(4), 1991, 94-6. Whitaker of Thornhill, 17th c.

WHITAKER, ROBERT SANDERSON. *Whitaker of Hesley Hall, Grayshott Hall, Pylewell Park and Palermo, being some family records ...* Mitchell Hughes and Clarke, 1907. Hesley Hall, Yorkshire; Grayshott Hall and Pylewell Park, Hampshire and Palermo, Italy. Includes pedigrees, medieval-19th c., with wills, monumental inscriptions, parish register extracts, *etc.,* concerning the Whitaker, Ingham, Fearnley, Sanderson, Blakiston, Jeans, Wakefield and Bennett families, medieval-19th c.

Whiteford

See Lovell

Whiteley

REDMONDS, GEORGE. 'Surname history: Whiteley', *H. & D.F.H.S.J.* 2(2), 1989, 55.
See also Pickles-Whiteley

Whiteman

See Wightman

Whiteoak

'Pedigree of Whiteoak of Lothersdale & Keighley', *K.D.F.H.S.J.* Winter 1993, 5. 19th c.

Whitfield

WASHBOURNE, C.M. 'Pedigree of Whitfield', *K.D.F.H.S.J.* Summer 1998, 14-15. 19-20th c.

Whitley

BRETTON, ROWLAND. 'The Whitleys of Halifax', *T.Hal.A.S.* 1963, 51-76. 18-20th c.

Whittaker

See Humble

Whittell

See Wilmer

Wickham

'Wickham', *Y.G.* **2**, 1890, 291-4. Pedigree, 16-19th c.

Widdrington

See Skeet

Wigglesworth

WIGGLESWORTH, GEORGE, & WIGGLESWORTH, MARGARET. 'Wigglesworth or Wrigglesworth?', *Y.F.H.* 18(4), 1992, 93-4. Note on the surname.

Wightman
I'ANSON, BRYAN. *Records of the Wightman (Whiteman or Weightman) family.* The author, 1917. Of Scotland, Leicestershire, Suffolk, Yorkshire *etc.,* medieval-20th c. Includes pedigrees, extracts form original sources, *etc.*

Wilberforce / Wilberfoss
WILBERFORCE-BELL, HAROLD. 'Some notes on the earlier history of the family of Wilberfoss of Wilberfoss', *Notes & queries* **194**, 1949, 136-9. Medieval-17th c.
'Table of descendants of Wm. Wilberforce, esq. M.P., *Y.N.Q.II.* **2**, 1906, 144-5. 18-20th c.

Wilby
See Skeet

Wild(e)
WILLIAMS, EILEEN. 'Striking lucky on the Wild (Wilde, Wyld, Wyl(de) side', *Y.F.H.* **23**(3), 1997, 73-7. Wild family, 18-19th c.

Wilkinson
'Wilkinsons of Lindley', *Y.F.H.* **15**(2), 1989, 41-3. Includes pedigree, 18-20th c.
See also Coates

Willcock
LEWIS, ENID. 'Willcock family history', *Don. Anc.* **6**(6), 1994, 142-3. 19th c. Of Pontefract and South Australia.

Willey
See

Williams
See

Williamson
CRAWLEY, MALCOM. 'My favourite ancestor: a story of two Williamsons (or three)', *Don. Anc.* **4**(4), 1990, 115-8. 18-19th c., includes notes on Etches family.

Willoughby
See Legard

Wilmer
FOSTER, CHARLES WILMER, & GREEN, JOSEPH J. *History of the Wilmer family, together with some account of its descendants.* Leeds: Goodall and Suddick, 1888. Includes chapters on 'Wilmer of Stratford le Bow, Bromley St. Leonards, Stifford and Barking; 'Green of London, Chalfont St. Giles, Saffron Walden and Stansted Montfichet ...', 'Watkins of Yorkshire', 'Field, Whittell and Herbert of Upper Helmsley... ', *etc.*

Wilson
ATTWOOD, GERTRUDE M. *The Wilsons of Tranby Croft.* Beverley: Hutton Press, 1988. 18-20th c.
CHAYTOR, M.H.F. *The Wilsons of Sharrow: the snuff makers of Sheffield.* Sheffield: J.W. Northend, 1962. 18-20th c., includes pedigree.
CROSSLAND, PHYLLIS. 'The Wilsons of Broomhead Hall', *Yorkshire history quarterly* **1**, 1995, 21-3. Includes brief pedigree, 14-20th c.
HUMPHERY-SMITH, C.R., & HEENAN, MICHAEL G. 'The ancestry of Mr. Harold Wilson', *Family history* **3**(17/18), 1965, 135-55. See also **4**(19), 1966, 13-14. Originally of Helmsley; 17-20th c., includes parish register extracts, 1851 census, list of wills, *etc.*
HUNTER, JOSEPH. 'A memoir on the origin, descent and alliances of the ancient family of Wilson of Bromhead, in the West Riding of the County of York, 1824', *Y.A.J.* **5**, 1879, 69-110. Includes pedigrees, 15-19th c.
REDMONDS, GEORGE. 'Surname history: Wilson', *H. & D.F.H.S.J.* **5**(3), 1992, 103.
WHEAT, JOHN B. 'Wilson of Broomhead', *T.Hunter A.S.* **3**, 1929, 53-65. Includes pedigrees, 13-18th c.
'Introductory note to memoirs on the Wilsons of Bromhead', *Y.A.J.* **4**, 1879, 63-4.
'The Wilson family', *Old Yorkshire* **4**, 1883, 242-3. Of Leeds, 17-18th c.
See also Blackburne

Wilton
'The Wiltons of Thorpe Audlin, Ackworth & Doncaster', *Don. Anc.* **7**(1), 1994, 26-8. 18-19th c.

Winter
See Roberts

Wint(e)ringham
BROUGHTON, DAVE. 'Beyond reasonable doubt', *Don. Anc.* **6**(6), 1994, 146-9. Winteringham family, 19th c.
NEALE, ELIZABETH F.W. 'From yeoman to court physician', *Genealogist magazine* **14**, 1964, 277-82. Wintringham of Belthorpe, 16-18th c.

Wise
'Wise of Appleton', *Y.G.* **2**, 1890, 75. Pedigree from an old bible, 17-18th c.

Wood(d)
WOOD, GEOFFREY WAINMAN. 'The Wood family of Leeds, 1800-1900', *Y.F.H.* **21**(1), 1995, 11-12.
KIDD, L.N. 'The Wood family of Saddleworth Fold, Heathfields and Spring Gardens', *B.S.H.S.* **15**(2), 1985, 27-30; **21**(2), 1991, 18-23. 18-19th c.
LEIGHTON, H R. 'A pedigree of the family of Wood of Egton, Aislaby and Whitby, in the County of York, and of South Shields in the County Palatine of Durham', *M.G.H.* 4th series **5**, 1913, 125-9. 17-19th c.
Pedigrees and memorials of the family of Woodd, formerly of Shynewood, Salop and Brize Norton, Oxfordshire; now of Conyngham Hall, Co. York, and Hampstead, Middlesex. Mitchell and Hughes, 1875. 15-19th c.
See also Mitchell

Woodlesford
See Wridlesford

Woodward
WOODWARD, FRANK HARRISON. *Woodwards of the Forest of Galtres: lucubrations.* York: [ ], 1970. Includes pedigrees, 16-20th c.

Wordsworth
ALDRED, HENRY W. 'Wordsworth of Water Hall', *Old Yorkshire* **8**, 1891, 202-6. 16-18th c., in Penistone.

BEDFORD, EDWIN JACKSON. *Genealogical memoranda relating to the family of Wordsworth.* Mitchell & Hughes, 1881. Includes pedigree, 15-18th c., and parish register extracts.
BEDFORD, EDWIN JACKSON. 'Pedigree of Wordsworth of Penistone, Co. York', *M.G.H.* N.S., **4**, 1884, 41-8. 14-18th c.
BEDFORD, EDWIN JACKSON. 'Extracts from the parish registers of Penistone, relating to the family of Wordsworth from 1644 to 1805', *M.G.H.* N.S., **3**, 1880, 402-4, 409-12 & 440-41.
WORDSWORTH, GORDON GRAHAM. *Some notes on the Wordsworths of Peniston and their aumbry.* Ambleside: St. Oswald Press, 1929. Includes pedigrees, 17-18th c.
'Extracts form the parish registers in the church of Silkstone, Co. York, relating to the family of Wordsworth', *M.G.H.* N.S., **4**, 1884, 9-12. Includes extracts from various other registers, with Silkstone monumental inscriptions.

Wormall
See Power

Wortley
CROSSLEY, PHYLLIS. 'The ancient family of Wortley', *Yorkshire history quarterly* **2**(1), 1996, 3-8. Includes pedigree, 16-20th c.
GROSVENOR, CAROLINE, & BEILBY, CHARLES. *The first Lady Wharncliffe and her family (1779-1856).* 2 vols. William Heinemann, 1927. Wortley and Henry families, includes pedigrees.

Wostenholm
BEXFIELD, HAROLD. *A short history of Sheffield cutlery and the house of Wostenholm.* Sheffield: Loxley Bros., 1945. 18-20th c.

Wray
WRAY, GEORGE OCTAVIUS. 'Family and pedigree of Wray', *Genealogist* **4**, 1880, 278-85. See also **5**, 1881, 141-2. 16-18th c.

Wridlesford
CLAY, C.T. 'The family of Wridlesford or Woodlesford', in *Miscellanea* **[8]**. *T.S.* **26**, 1924, 243-52. 12-13th c.; of Woodlesford.

Wrigglesworth
See Wigglesworth

Wright
See Rodes

Wrightson
DALLAS, JAMES. 'Family of Wrightson', *Genealogist* **3**, 1879, 400-402. 18th c.

Wyat
BODDINGTON, REGINALD STEWART. 'Family of Wyat', *M.G.H.* N.S., **2**, 1877, 106-8. Of Yorkshire, Kent, *etc.,* 16-19th c.

Wykeham
See Atkinson

Wyld(e)
See Wild(e)

Wyndham
See Rawlins

Yarker
YARKER, JOHN. *Genealogy of the surname Yarker, with the Leyburn and several allied families resident in the counties of Yorkshire, Durham, Westmorland, and Lancashire, including all of the name in Cumberland, Canada, America, and Middlesex.* Manchester: A.M. Petty & Co., 1882. Includes extensive pedigrees, medieval-19th c.

'Family of Yarker', *Y.G.* **1**, 1888, 105-8. 15-19th c.
'The Yarker family of Yorkshire', *M.G.H.* N.S., **1**, 1874, 153-6. Parish register extracts from Wensley and Barton, Yorkshire, and from Morland, Westmorland, *etc.,* 16-18th c.

York(e)
MOORE, D.G. 'Memoirs concerning Sir Richard York (of York), knight (obit A.D. 1498) and the ancient stained glass of a memorial window, formerly in the church of St. John the Evangelist, Ousebridge End, in the City of York ...', *Y.A.J.* **37**, 1951, 213-20. Includes will.
COOPER, ANNE ASHLEY. *Yorke county.* Hexton: the author, 1988. Yorke family, 15-20th c.

Youle
REYNOLDS, HY. FITZGERALD. 'Youle of Co. Yorks', *Notes & queries* **165**, 1933, 277-8. See also 339. 19th c., includes will of Edward Youle of Stainforth, 1805.

Author Index

Family Name Index

IMPORTANT

This is an index to sections 1 to 5 only; it does not include the numerous names listed in section 6. Since the latter are in alphabetical order, it would be superfluous to include them here.

Place Name Index